WHATEVER IT TAKES

Sangeetha Chakrapani is the founder of Together Foundation that works towards empowering people with autism and special needs and The Together Community, a residential project for people with autism, their friends and families. This is Sangeetha's first book.

Sangeetha Chakrapani

WHATEVER IT TAKES

AUTISM, PARENTING AND A DREAM

WESTLAND NON·FICTION

WESTLAND
NON·FICTION

Published by Westland Non-Fiction, an imprint of Westland Books, a division of Nasadiya Technologies Private Limited, in 2026

No. 269/2B, First Floor, 'Irai Arul', Vimalraj Street, Nethaji Nagar, Alapakkam Main Road, Maduravoyal, Chennai 600095

Westland, the Westland logo, Westland Non-Fiction and the Westland Non-Fiction logo are the trademarks of Nasadiya Technologies Private Limited, or its affiliates.

Copyright © Sangeetha Chakrapani, 2026

Sangeetha Chakrapani asserts the moral right to be identified as the author of this work.

ISBN: 9789371970891

10 9 8 7 6 5 4 3 2 1

The views and opinions expressed in this work are the author's own and the facts are as reported by her, and the publisher is in no way liable for the same.

All rights reserved

Typeset by Mukul Chand

Printed at Thomson Press India Private Limited

No part of this book may be reproduced, or stored in a retrieval system, or transmitted in any form or by any means, electronic, mechanical, photocopying, recording, or otherwise, without express written permission of the publisher.

Thanksgiving
*With humble salutations at the lotus feet of Sri Sathya Sai Baba,
I offer my gratitude to:
My parents, S. Lakshiminarayanan and Mythili
Facebook for giving writers instant glory
Meher Pestonjee for teaching me to write for myself
Kiran Khalap for asking me to write four books, which left me
bemused but also awash with the sunshine of confidence that I have
a story to tell*

Contents

Prologue — xi

1. 'That is your story, Sangeetha' — 1
2. Before the children — 5
3. 'Let's see how many babies you are going to have' — 12
4. 'When I woke up, I was a mother!' — 21
5. Going home with the babies! — 27
6. How could I be depressed? — 33
7. Stumbling towards childhood — 46
8. Growing up … together — 54
9. Dreams come true … at a price — 68
10. Scraping through as a family — 79
11. Jai Rajinikanth! — 82

Epilogue — 85

Margazhi Stories — 87

Children

My children
tore my womb
made my world asunder
Shock. Fear. Questions. More questions.

Smaller than a bird's bum
Skin softer than marshmallows
Pink. Wrinkled. Helpless.
Me too
Helpless.

Alone
Where are
my four children
Looking down my stomach
Why is it empty suddenly?

Alone
Praying ghostlike
Unsmiling. Bloated. Unloved.
Doing what I must.
Alone for a long time.

x Children

My children talk to me.
Laugh and compel me.
Fountains burst, waterfalls
gush down
Spring!

Courage
Head rises
No more fear!
I will live again.
Live with my children again!

Prologue

YOU COME HOME ONE EVENING.
While patiently waiting outside our grille gate to be let in, you are likely to see a moon-faced girl. Jayanthi will look at you enquiringly, like Mother Duck, her head slightly turned in one direction. And just when you think she is going to open the door, she will walk away, leaving you bleating, 'Open the door.' If you see a young lady of ample proportions tumbling towards you like a baby elephant, it is Lakshmi.

Then come the social introductions. We have a strict policy at home while introducing Lakshmi and Jayanthi. Introduce *only once*, and give them enough time to process and respond. If they don't respond, we just amble along.

Say hi, say hello, uncle ko hello bolo, shake hands karo, give a high five—these are an absolute no-no. Lakshmi and Jayanthi are quite comfortable and they sit quietly in the living room, perfectly at ease, making *no* attempt at conversation.

But what about you, the visitor? Here you are in the living room of a family with four young adults, two of whom you have no clue how to connect with. Questions like 'How are you?' will get a staccato, 'I am fine', or a thumbs up. In fact, Lakshmi goes one step further. 'Hello, how are you, I am fine, how are you, I am fine, thank you,' she goes the whole hog. Then, relieved to have got it out of the way, she settles down.

That's when, while sitting on one of our clunky sofas, your face brightens as you see the unmistakable, unmissable, jumbo-size carrom board right in the middle of the centre table, with a big plastic container of coins. You inch forward hopefully. 'I like playing carrom too,' you say, and open the box of coins.

Jayanthi's eyes brighten and she takes a place. Lakshmi rushes inside to get talcum powder, which she then proceeds to sprinkle generously on the board.

'Er ... enough, Lakshmi,' you say.

You take the first chance and play. Jayanthi keeps looking at you till you say, 'Jayanthi, will you play with me?'

Lakshmi, unasked, shoots off a coin, disregarding all rules of the game. But you don't mind. Oh no, not at all! You look at her admiringly while, out of the corner of your eye, you see Jayanthi still looking at you anxiously.

'Play, Jayanthi!'

Then Jayanthi inches forward and, ever so hesitantly, puts her thumb and index finger together.

That's it! The windows of autism open, and the many-splendoured winds of friendship waft in. Taking pleasure in doing simple and uncomplicated things together that don't require you to ask: What is your name? How old are you? What are you doing? What are your plans?

Eventually, our trademark lemon tea makes its way to the table. I make my presence felt with a plateful of eatables. Jayanthi continues to play while looking at you anxiously. You continue giving her permission to play. Lakshmi continues to interpret the carrom board freely. You continue looking at her admiringly. Krishna prevents Lakshmi and Jayanthi from waltzing off. Jayashree feels like she is Vasco da Gama, for having thought of getting a carrom board.

CP looks on with a proprietary air: *This is my family. See how nicely they are playing carrom with a visitor? See how civilised we are? It was I who gave permission for this giant carrom board to be placed bang in the middle of the hall, provided we stop depositing things like water bottles, plates and cups around it.*

1
'That is your story, Sangeetha'

ANDAL, BORN IN THE EIGHTH CENTURY IN THE VILLAGE OF Srivilliputhur in Tamil Nadu, was the daughter of the temple priest. It was the young girl's duty to string flowers into a garland for the deity every day. When Andal's father found that she was wearing the garland herself before offering it to the deity, he rebuked her. But the Lord appeared and accepted her garland.

Andal's fervour for Lord Krishna resulted in the magnificent composition *Thiruppavai*, a set of thirty verses in chaste Tamil, describing the journey of a devotee towards Krishna. Every year, from 16 December to 14 January, in the wee hours of the morning, *Thiruppavai* is chanted in homes, in small processions on the streets and in temples. This period is called Margazhi.

CP and I were married in the month of September. In December, my father-in-law said to me, 'Sangeetha, Margazhi will begin in a few days. Please draw a simple kolam and light two lamps at the entrance to the home, early in the morning before 5.30 a.m.'

I took his request seriously and produced the traditional rangoli to the best of my ability. They turned out unwieldy, yes, but my father-in-law encouraged my efforts and my mother-in-law laboured to repair them.

By my second Margazhi in 2003, I was pregnant. From then on, life changed irrevocably. Four babies entered our lives at the same time, marking the beginning of a tumultuous and life-changing parenting experience. Children requiring surgeries for congenital issues. Children requiring intervention for disorders that cannot be resolved. Knowing that our children will never be like others. Learning to be parents again and again.

Over the years, as the children grew up, the tumult in our lives swelled like a river in flood. The raging waters of distress and shock stripped us of the outer veneer of a happy family. It took nine years for us to learn that love, affection, festivals, holidays and other normal things can go hand in hand with autism. Like a warrior who realises that he is never complete without his battle gear, like a soldier who feels naked without his arms and ammunition, CP and I started carrying autism like the clothes on our backs.

In 2011, when the children were nine years old, I started a new tradition: I would draw kolams for Margazhi and write a story on Facebook about my family for every kolam that I drew. People enjoyed reading about the experiences of the children, CP and me. These 'Margazhi stories' converted our imperfections, our struggles and our small victories into rays of hope for ourselves and for others.

I would wake up at approximately three in the morning, have a bath, light the lamp, draw the rangoli, take a photo and then sit down to write. My mind would wander as I wrote, and an episode would assert itself in my memory. Sometimes the humour would assert itself, sometimes the pain. Often, I would draw the rangoli after writing the story. The kolams were as unconventional as my stories. I always draw one for each of my children as per their nicknames: Elephant, Tomato, Squirrel and Butterfly. I have drawn a park, a parrot, a teddy bear and even a shop, depending on the story.

This ritual of writing Margazhi stories became my reawakening. As I wrote the stories, I introspected and realised that we are a very strong family. We have stuck by each other and never given up. I saw the same realisation dawning on CP and the children as they woke up each morning and read something about themselves.

While writing this book, I wondered how I could include the Margazhi stories in the narration. These stories are incidents that reflect the growing up of a family. Incidents that made us laugh, cry, lean on each other, seek help and sometimes questioned our faith in ourselves and each other. The are windows into the life of our family. Over the years, readers have found these stories easy to read and connect with; they laugh, shed a few tears or mull over them. These stories are like an assorted potluck of dishes with multiple flavours which one can dip into. They appear as a separate section in the later part of the book. I hope they'll serve as a reminder that there is hope, a silver lining, or that life is beautiful despite everything.

~

I did not take my writings seriously till Kiran Khalap called me to his office and proceeded to stun me with his words.

'Write four books, Sangeetha. One on every child.'

I've known Kiran for years, since I was a novice and he the CEO of Clarion Advertising.

I met him for the first time in 1996, on a bus journey to Naukuchiatal. We were going to attend a workshop about creativity. He sat next to me and listened to stories of my love for animals. I woke up early next morning and what do I find? Kiran atop a tree with a bunch of children! The image made me think of a modern-day gurukul. I knew right away that this man would always be part of my life.

Nineteen years later, Kiran was in Mumbai. He had founded a brand consultancy firm called chlorophyll. CP, the kids and I travelled to Nariman Point from Andheri East to meet him, carrying juice and tumblers since our daughters with autism don't drink from glasses. Kiran did not bat an eyelid when we proceeded to convert his conference room into an Udupi-style tearoom, complete with steel tumblers.

After we settled down with our juices, I asked Kiran to help us start a business that could be run by my children with autism. He wore the robes of a corporate honcho, the cap of a mind reader, the heart of Amul Butter, the soul of a saint, and proceeded to shepherd us to planet Together Foundation.

With Kiran's soul-stirring mission statement embedded in my heart and mind, I began the task of shaping the work of Together Foundation, a registered public charitable trust that would go beyond academics and offer a canvas of learning opportunities to young adults with autism and special needs.

In seven years, the foundation has grown from a team of only Lakshmi and Jayanthi to one of thirty-five adults. Today, it has a bakery certified by the Food Safety and Standards Authority of India (FSSAI), a manufacturing unit that produces eco-friendly products, a registered shop in the premises, and a training centre for imparting computer and data entry skills for financial institutions. We conduct life-skills training programmes that teach personal hygiene, alternative and augmentative communication, the use of social media and how to shop. We have a family counselling centre and we support parents as they plan their children's transition towards independent living. We have also launched our dream project of a residential space called The Together Community at Hosur, where people with autism will live independently and safely in a supportive environment even after the lifetime of their parents.

∼

When Kiran proposed that I write four books, I said, 'Kiran, I have not made things happen. Things have happened to me. How can I behave as if I did something great or unique?'

'Sangeetha, yes, things happened, but what matters is what you did when those things happened,' he said. 'When you faced huge problems, you did not give up. You started doing small, positive things. You chipped away at the mountain till small, positive things started happening. That is your story, Sangeetha, and you need to share it.'

2
Before I became a mother

My father, S. Lakshiminarayanan, was thirty-three years old when he married the twenty-three-year-old Mythili. To this day, Jayashree and Krishna can't understand how their grandmother, and then their mother, married men much older than themselves. Every time CP wants to wring some respect from me, he reminds me he's eleven years older than me!

My father started out as an agricultural trainee at the age of nineteen for a salary of ninety rupees a month and retired as vice-president of Chambal Fertilisers, a K.K. Birla company. He was the oldest of ten siblings and grew up in a home run on spartan means. His father was a jail superintendent. As his mother he had an indomitable woman who gave him the resilience to shoulder responsibilities at a young age.

My mother was born in a small village in Tamil Nadu. Despite her family's economic challenges, her thirst for reading and education was fulfilled. She worked as a teacher, ran her own school and wrote stories with an indefatigable spirit till her last day on earth.

My father had a transferable job, which meant our family constantly moved between cities. My elder sister Vaidehi was born in Orissa. It was after her birth that my family moved to Hubli where I was born two years later, in 1972. The next stop was Hyderabad, where I studied at Keyes High School from Class I to Class IV. The school had the kindest environment. It had teachers who did up your hair for you if it came loose, and spoke with you in Tamil and Telugu. St. Mary's School in Poona, where I studied from Class V to Class VIII, had children who looked at my oily hair with unease, teachers who looked down impossibly long noses, and friends who lasted for only two days when they realised that I did not know the difference between 'there' and 'their'.

By the time I found my best friend, Harini, at St. Mary's, I was in Class VIII and it was time to move to Sharada Mandir High School, Goa. I had begun my lifelong love affair with the English language, thanks to my father who helped me write an essay titled 'The Autobiography of a Diamond' for a school assignment. I marvelled at my father's imagery and fluid expression of thought. I swam and gloried in the sylvan waters of the English language and to this day can recite *Ode to a Skylark* by Percy Bysshe Shelley and *Le Morte d'Arthur* by Alfred Lord Tennyson.

Our next move was to Delhi where I graduated in English Honours from Jesus and Mary College and found my lifelong mentor in Sister (Dr) Melba Rodrigues. To this day, whenever I visit her, I find it hard to leave the quiet and serenity of the convent and return to my world.

My first job was as a marketing trainee at BPL Home Appliances, at a time when microwaves were being launched in India. I was always fascinated by brand management and advertising and would voraciously read any books on the subjects I could lay my hands on. I worked for a few years in Lintas and Clarion Advertising in New Delhi.

The tumultuous years began after my sister Vaidehi married and left home to build her nest with Raghavan, a chartered accountant by profession. Though Vaidehi was just a call away, Amma, Appa and I missed her terribly. The train journey back from Tirupati, where her wedding had taken place, was a gloomy one, with the three of us smiling brightly at one another and making forced conversation as if a piece of our hearts had not been separated and taken away from us that very day.

This was the time I got married and went through a divorce. My parents had engaged in an intensive bridegroom hunt, searching high and low, hither and thither, but the marriage lasted only six months, and both the young man and I scuttled back into our respective nests as fast as we could. Today, I am able to share this with equanimity, but in those days, I was shaken and tossed by the winds of sorrow. If only I had said 'No' and stuck to it.

I moved to Bangalore while my parents stayed in Chennai. I lived in a tiny room as a paying guest. My room had a large window that faced the quiet Cox Town railway station. I found a job at Lintas and would scurry back to the security of my room after work. A home library and the nearby Murugan temple were my refuge on weekends. I would sit by the window for hours, watching the trains chug past, imagining the travellers, their stories, their journeys. How odd these two journeys are: one that we pay for with our own lives and yet have no idea where it is taking us, and the other that we pay a handful of money for but have full knowledge of its exact route and destination. I am sure I must have been Meena Kumari in my previous life as a train always strikes at my soul as it does hers in the iconic *Pakeezah*.

Amma was unstoppable and began to advise me to go out, meet people, make friends. I realised that she was hoping for a live demonstration of a Mills & Boon romance in my life. I was immersed in two things only: my love for animals and my intense attraction to god and temples. I had begun working in animal rescue, fulfilling my craving to care for animals. I had a beautiful clay idol of baby Krishna that I had procured from the bewitching Navaneetha Krishna temple at Channapatna, Mysore. This idol became the receptacle of my adoration and even today, the temple draws me like a magnet.

It was at this point that Amma and Appa engineered a meeting with CP.

CP won my mother's undivided affection from day one. I met him and felt like a rose trying to grow in the same pot as the *Welwitschia mirabilis*, the world's toughest plant. I did not hesitate for a second; it was a no for me. My mother refused to speak to me and my father maintained a steely silence.

Over the course of the next two years, CP kept in touch with me through greeting cards that my mother faithfully stored. In this interim period, he engineered a visit to Mumbai for me, to see his home and meet his parents. It would help me overcome my fear of the unknown, he told my father. When I met CP in Mumbai, accompanied by my father, the force of his personality had not dimmed. But then, neither had my reaction.

We had a long conversation, at the end of which I told him I needed time.

'How much time?' he asked.

'A year.'

'Absolutely not! Please decide and say yes now.'

His mother beckoned me into the kitchen. A thrifty, simple-hearted and vivacious lady, she had shifted from Kumbakonam in interior Tamil Nadu to Mumbai more than four decades earlier. Draped in a nine-yard saree, she had embraced Mumbai and struck lasting friendships with a gamut of people ranging from the chaiwala to CP's colleagues.

Eyes swimming with tears, she asked me, 'Why are you saying no? Are you scared?'

'Yes,' I said.

'We are all scared of him,' she said simply. 'But he is a good man. He has taken care of all of us since a young age. He is not one son. He is a hundred sons.'

Startled by her conviction, I smiled shakily and left the kitchen.

On my return to Bangalore, CP called me.

'Have you made up your mind?' he asked.

'Yes.'

'Then I want you to note down this date in your diary as the day you made the most memorable mistake of your life.'

I gasped and called up my dad who sounded pleased and proud.

A year passed and I decided to move back to Chennai. I had secured a job in the marketing department of Bisleri. Their office was a stone's throw from my parents' place and I was looking forward to returning home.

I reached home to a happy welcome from my parents and grandmother. My grandmother always looked at me with a healthy suspicion since I was not one of the happily married ladies of the family. I logged into my email and gave a little jump. It was CP, tersely asking for my phone number. I hastily logged out without replying. I had to go back to Bangalore the same night, to attend a meeting that the police commissioner had called for. The meeting was about street dogs. When I returned from Bangalore, my mother opened the door with a wide smile. My father looked as if he had won a lottery. Even my grandmother smiled at me.

Suspicion rose like a fountain.

'Amma, what is the excitement all about?' I asked.

'I prayed and sent him to you. He has come.'

Supremely irritating words, but now that I am a mother, I can understand.

My parents were aghast that I had not had the civility to respond to CP's email. He, in turn, had called my father.

～

They say marriages are made in heaven. Ours was made over a single phone call. CP called, I answered, and found myself agreeing to marry him. It was a sort of breaking down of all barriers in spite of his gravitas and resounding seriousness and my happy-as-a-lark persona.

When we married, he was vice president of the audit and compliance department at HDFC Bank and I was a passionate animal lover who had run a twenty-four-hour ambulance for street animals. I knew that our marriage was for better or worse, and we have not been spared either of the experiences in the twenty years and more that we have spent together.

~

My father-in-law was a man of austere habits. His one overwhelming passion in life was Carnatic music which he had taught himself. '*Vandanamo raghu nandana*,' he would sing with hands folded in front of the altar, voice shaking with age and emotion. My shopping trips were a source of anxiety and bafflement to him. He was also concerned about my intense interest in prayer. 'You have to align yourself with family life, Sangeetha,' he once told me.

As CP and I struggled to understand one another, my parents-in-law moved out into a small apartment called Rose View. Beset by guilt, I would visit them often and find peace in their simple, uncomplicated company. In those initial years of our marriage, all the space in the Amazon forest could not have closed the wide chasm between CP and me. It would take much more than the needless moving out of my in-laws for the two of us to walk together, hand in weary hand.

My mother-in-law passed away when the children were barely three years old. I had not attempted to know her better, and by the time wisdom dawned, it was too late. She was gone. What remains is a lasting regret.

When my father-in-law passed away in Bangalore in 2010, I was alone with him in hospital. The nurses called me. 'He won't be there for long. Please inform his children.'

I hastily called CP and went back inside.

My father-in-law was lying down with his eyes closed and I cradled his head on my lap. I bent and pressed my lips to his forehead. He was cold. He had gone. I took an auto and went home. It was pouring, ice rained down and competed with the tears rolling down my face. His room lay waiting. All his worldly belongings fitted inside a small briefcase and there was still some space left.

CP reached Bangalore that evening and stood stoically to give his father the final farewell. I had to persuade him to sit by my side and hold his father, to express the sorrow that undeniably lay beneath his granite exterior.

3
'Let's see how many babies you are going to have'

OUR NEIGHBOURHOOD GYNAECOLOGIST WAS TIRED OF MY repeated visits to her clinic.

'Sangeetha, you got married in September and expected to become pregnant in October. Now, you already suspect a problem!'

Finally, she gave in and asked me to get a sonography. The test revealed that I had one of the most common problems of the modern era: polycystic ovarian disorder, a medical condition that causes irregular menstrual cycles, hair loss, abnormal weight gain—and infertility.

I lost no time in consulting a well-known fertility specialist, in South Bombay, who recommended intrauterine insemination, or IUI. And I decided to go ahead.

It was a two-hour journey from our home in Andheri East to the fertility clinic, a trip that I took alone on the first day of the treatment. I was pale with anxiety as I stepped into the clinic. The clinic was strangely empty. A tall and gaunt nurse came towards me.

'Doctor is not available. She is seriously unwell and hospitalised. Don't worry, her assistant will give the injection.'

This injection was meant to induce ovulation.

The next day, the assistant doctor, too, was missing from action.

'Doctor is busy. She has told me to give you the injection,' the nurse informed me.

The oil-based injection was given in the thigh and I was asked to run an ice pack over it. A few minutes into our ride back home, we passed an old temple. 'This is Babulnath mandir. It is a very powerful temple,' our driver, Anil, told me.

I asked him to stop, walked up the long flight of stairs, worshipped and came back.

For the next twenty days, my treatment was run solely by the nurse. She would administer the injection. On our way back, we would stop over at the temple—it was like a ritual. Years later, on 19 January 2009, I visited the temple again, this time with CP and our children. It was the quadruplets' fifth birthday.

The quickness with which I had plunged into the treatment plan had stumped CP. He was taken aback by my militant desire to experience motherhood, and it had led to a fragile silence between us.

One day, at around 8.30 a.m., after I had finished cooking, given CP his lunch box and packed the lunch for my in-laws that he would deliver on his way to work, I realised I had left the front door open.

As I walked towards it, I sank to the floor. Pain was coming in big grinding waves.

My helper, Ashwini, walked in, took one look at me, and helped me get to the local gynaecologist's clinic four buildings away. Within fifteen minutes, Tramazac, a painkiller injection, was administered to me. In the months to come, when I was being treated for what was diagnosed as ovarian hyperstimulation, I would beg the nurses in vain to give me that injection.

My neighbourhood gynaecologist was appalled when I told her about the missing doctor and assistant doctor. She referred us to several hospitals for further treatment.

Looking back, I see that I did not use my common sense. If we go to a hospital for treatment and the doctor is not there, will we allow a nurse to decide on a treatment, even if she offers to? Will we not insist on the doctor? Plus, the fertility treatment was not an emergency. How could I allow a nurse to administer me a highly specialised treatment rather than telling her I'd wait for the doctor to return?

Over the next decade and a half, I was to interact with a galaxy of doctors, surgeons and other members of the medical fraternity. First, I contacted a reputable fertility specialist and put myself in her care. After the children were born, I went on to consult multiple specialists for various problems relating to raising four young children of the same age simultaneously, autism intervention and possible treatments, Krishna's surgeries and so on. This made me realise that doctors are completely human. Even the best surgeons make unintentional mistakes, and it is a matter of great luck and destiny to find the right doctor.

But at that time, after the neighbourhood gynaecologist's referrals, CP escorted me to a well-known gynaecologist in South Bombay. CP and I had decided that I would go to Breach Candy Hospital or look for another doctor.

CP had been making decisions for himself and his family from a very young age. His parents, particularly my mother-in-law, believed he was a fine blend of Sage Agastya and the iconic Rajinikanth. While I did not enjoy the same reputation with my parents, my sister and I had been raised to be highly independent people.

Decision-making was not an alien concept for CP and me. But the baby project certainly was.

We entered the hallowed precincts of Breach Candy Hospital. Because of overstimulation of the ovarian follicles, my stomach had become distended with water. I could not eat even one piece of bread. I had to undergo four aspirations to remove the excess water. When the long needle first went into my abdomen, I shrieked so much that nurses from the adjoining wards came rushing in. The doctors looked shaken; one of the nurses hastily drew the curtains and closed every door so that the other patients would not get rattled. Four to five litres of water was removed during every aspiration. What a relief it was! After every aspiration, I was ravenous and ate a full meal. However, within a day, the water retention would begin again and the misery would increase steadily over a week, till the next aspiration was done.

Resplendent in rich Kanjeevaram sarees, the gynaecologist was an imposing lady. She would meet me for a couple of minutes during her daily rounds. After a few days, I told her that I was feeling better. She smiled, patted my shoulder and said, 'Good, now let's see how many babies you are going to have.'

Somewhere in the middle of this ceaseless anguish, a pregnancy test was quietly done and I was confirmed pregnant.

Do you remember all those movies where husbands and wives share that special joy of knowing that they are going to become parents? They gaze into each other's eyes forever, with peacocks dancing in the background and pigeons cooing nonstop. When I called CP to share the news, he was driving towards the hospital. 'Yes, very good,' he replied, tersely.

That was it. The pregnancy celebration was over.

Once my pregnancy was confirmed, the sonography was carried out: a minor event by itself. I was shifted out of Breach Candy and taken to a private clinic. A sonologist with decades of experience had been specially requested to carry out my test. As I lay on the table and the instrument rotated slowly across my abdomen, I saw his face assume a sickly grey colour. He stopped the instrument, reapplied the gel, and swiped the device across my abdomen again.

He looked pale.

I felt a wave of compassion for him. *Maybe I am not pregnant at all and he is wondering how to tell me*, I thought. So I went ahead and did what I always do—I voiced my opinion to the medical professional before he could pronounce his views. Now, this is a habit that CP deplores. To this day, he alternates between pleading with me and counselling me, 'Sangeetha, kindly let the doctor speak before you tell him what you think he should say.'

'Doctor, it's okay if I am not pregnant,' I said. 'Please tell me. I can deal with it.'

'It's not that, beta. You are carrying four babies.'

I was elated that I was pregnant. Plus, I have always wanted a big family. My concern was more for my mother, who swayed, clutched at the table and quickly exited the room to tell Appa. Husband, friend, mentor, guru, my father was everything and more to my mother. By the time I was escorted out of the sonography room, clucked over by a battery of nurses who treated me as if I was Mother India about to go into labour, CP had arrived.

As I entered the waiting room, I saw CP with his head bent towards my parents, listening to them. They were gesturing with anxiety and CP looked as agitated as a freshly washed cucumber. In the coming years, I would understand that both CP and I possess a startling similarity in facing challenges head on. Before I could even talk to CP, the doctors called us in. They trod cautiously.

'You know, Mrs Chakrapani, there was an Iranian sportswoman who we treated with IUI. She was more than six feet tall and she could not carry twins to term. Ma'am, you are less than five feet tall.'

I looked at them in alarm and disbelief. What exactly were they trying to say?

'Foetal reduction. We will save the two healthiest babies and let the other two babies go.'

I argued and argued against it and then was gently taken home.

CP did not say a word to me. Amma and Appa were decidedly in favour of reduction as they had been told that there was also a risk to my life.

The silence in the car was deafening, and the decision had been made without words. I was to go home and take complete bed rest for fourteen days. On the fifteenth day, I was to be admitted to the hospital for foetal reduction.

My fourteen days of bed rest went by in a sea of trauma. On the thirteenth day, my parents were watching TV and I had been resting on the bed in my room. CP was in Chennai and was to return the next day. When I got up to pick up a book, I noticed there was a sea of blood on the floor. I called Breach Candy Hospital.

'Come right now, you understand? Immediately!'

I called Anil to drive us to the hospital. I tried to mop the floor with a bedsheet under my feet, not wanting my parents to see the blood. Anil rang the bell and that's when I told Amma and Appa that we had to leave for the hospital.

Both reacted with admirable calm as they got ready to travel with me from Andheri East to Breach Candy Hospital. It took close to two hours and the hospital must have called at least four times as we made our way there.

As we drew up to the imposing driveway of the famous hospital, I recognised one of the doctors standing outside with a stretcher, onto which they quickly shifted me. A sonography machine had been placed in a room at the entrance of the hospital and the test was immediately done.

By this time, all concepts of delicacy and privacy had become non-existent. Around twenty people, including my father, were standing inside. There was a gasp of relief as the doctor exclaimed, 'All the babies are fine!' And then there was a louder collective gasp as the doctor said, 'Wait! I think there's a fifth baby in here.'

'Fifth baby!' I exclaimed.

'Shut up, Sangeetha!' my father shouted in a quavering voice.

Then we heard the sonologist's gentle laugh. 'No, I am sorry. I was mistaken.'

The bleeding continued for five months, leaving the doctors and consultants bewildered. The hospital bills were mounting and made me realise how foolish I had been in asking for a single room. I called CP. 'Please shift me to a two-patient room.' A week later, I shifted to a four-patient room.

At the end of approximately four and a half months, I was sent home for around two weeks. The doctors had also opined that this time they would take a chance and go ahead with the foetal reduction.

The demons came back in full form.

Back home, I called up several hospitals in Delhi, where I had lived for seven years. I called up two reputable hospitals in Chennai and spoke to the gynaecologists there. I asked them at what stage of life my babies were. I wept and wept as they described that by the fifth month, the bones, the eyes and the limbs are all formed. I called up the nuns at two convents in Mumbai and asked them if they would take me in, if my family refused to support me. One of them said an unconditional yes. The other asked me to wait.

That night, when CP returned home from work, I did not wait for him to freshen up. I told him everything I had done. 'Everything will happen the way you want it to,' he said.

Managing the pregnancy at home was a nightmare. A doctor had to come home every day to check my heartbeat and blood pressure. Portable sonography machines had to be carted to our home. An ambulance had to be called to drive me to my weekly check-up at the hospital. Half the building would be out to see me go for my check-up. The babies had started kicking. I had the most unreasonable fears. I called the hospital after midnight and asked, 'The kicking is fierce; I hope the babies won't just come out on their own?'

'Mrs Chakrapani, go to sleep.'

I had to use a portable toilet and an ayah was recruited to clean up. This ignominy began from day one of my pregnancy and continued till I gave birth to the babies. Today, after helping toilet train four babies, I remember the ayahs who carried out this unpleasant task for me and feel a wave of gratitude for the cheerful attitude they brought to their job. I could not get into or out of bed without help. I was not allowed to bathe every day. I flatly refused that diktat and sat in a chair, wearing my nightgown. The ayah poured soap water on me and then fresh water. Also, the bleeding miraculously stopped at this juncture.

I vividly remember one of the trips I made by ambulance from Andheri East to Grant Road for the weekly check-up. I was so tired that I felt I would fall unconscious. I needed to get a bed under me. On the way back home, I started pointing out various hotels to CP.

'Let's just take a room and sleep here,' I raved and ranted at him.

But he drove the car home, grim-faced and iron jawed. When I got out of the car, I leaned against a column in the parking area, unable to move, weeping with exhaustion. He put me in the wheelchair, helped me into the lift and got me into bed. Job done.

Today, I realise the enormous responsibility of ensuring my safety that CP carried. I also learnt that he had booked a bed for me in at least three hospitals on the way from Andheri East to Grant Road in case an untoward event occurred en route.

The doctor had decided that my caesarean would take place at Bombay Hospital and that's where I was sent when my homestay ended. We had mounted enormous hospital bills by then and I asked to be accommodated in the general ward.

The fifth month onwards, anxiety for the babies shot up in all of us. We had also been warned that all four babies may require ventilator support. I had a memorable chat on the phone with a senior medical professional at the Bombay Hospital paediatric ward.

'Yes, Mrs Chakrapani?'

'You see, I am pregnant with quadruplets and will be getting admitted any time now. I wanted to know what arrangements we should make in case all four babies require ventilator support.'

'How many months along are you, Mrs Chakrapani?'

'Five months, doctor.'

'Please do not plan anything till you cross seven months.'

Click.

That day, I took out a small notebook and started writing 'Sri Rama Jayam' twenty-one times every day till the day the children were born. I had a massive book with copious notes of multifaith prayers sent to me by various well-wishers.

When my pregnancy touched seven months, the team at the Bombay Hospital NICU stepped in. I was so happy. At least now they believed that I would give birth to the babies. They started examining me every day. The trainees vied to examine me and

I would help them locate the four heartbeats as they took the monitor round and round my abdomen.

CP made the decision to purchase a larger flat. He tried to talk to me about it when he visited the hospital. But I had a single-track mind and would wave him away. 'Do whatever you want.' At no point did I extend any emotional support to him. All I could think of were the babies.

Having grown up with extreme financial hardship in his adolescence and early adult years, CP's strongest memories of childhood are not of holidays or a special set of clothes or outings. They are of his close-knit family and the homely atmosphere of the chawl he lived in. They are of simple stays in the hamlet of Karaikudi at Tamil Nadu to be with his sister. They are of weekend shopping expeditions with his father and brother to find a fridge at the cheapest price, and of helping his mother make sweets for Diwali to share with all the neighbours. These experiences have helped him stay grounded and retain his simplicity even after he made a much more comfortable life for himself.

At the end of December, my doctor visited me.

'Sangeetha, I am travelling for two weeks and in case it's required, your caesarean will be done by another doctor.'

But I defied all expectations till the doctor returned from her vacation. A sonography was carried out. One baby was growing at a far slower pace than the others. My prayers became more fervent and I began negotiations with the divine. This underweight baby was named Krishna before birth.

The doctor visited me in the afternoon. I was alone and uneasily resting. 'The weakest baby has stopped growing in the womb. We need to operate soon. Let's see, today is the seventeenth. I will operate on the nineteenth.'

With a swish of her Kanjeevaram saree, she was gone. I called CP, my parents and in-laws in excitement.

4
When I woke up, I was a mother!

19 January 2004. CP reached the hospital early in the morning. So did my dad. One of the interns approached me. 'Doctor wants to know if we can record the birth. We've never had a quadruplet delivery before this.'

'I don't mind even if you call the watchman in. Just give me my babies safely.'

That's when I realised that the operation theatre was full: medical students, interns and resident doctors. Something like the first day, first show of a Rajinikanth movie. The doctor walked in and gave everyone an icy look. Miraculously, the room cleared of more than half its occupants.

Three anaesthetists were present. The procedure was explained to me. When I woke up, I was a mother! I clamoured to see the babies, cleaned myself up as best as I could and was wheeled to the NICU. Sister Lalee, the nurse in charge, let me in. She gently took away the eye pencil I had been clutching in my hand. Just one dot, I begged. She smiled and gave it back to me. As I entered the NICU, the overpowering smell of Sterillium hit me—a smell that, to this day, makes my throat close and brings back memories of my newborn babies.

Sister Lalee took me to one section of the NICU and waved her hand.

'Sangeetha, all the babies in this room are yours.'

I could hear the incessant hum and ticking of the monitors.

'Where is the fourth baby?' I asked.

She pointed to a large incubator with a tiny baby inside, hooked to a ventilator. The kindest thing I could say about the baby was that he looked somewhat like a baby. His face was lined with wrinkles, his head was enormous and his body tiny. So, this was Krishna. My first reaction was one of unmitigated alarm: how am I going to raise this child?

The babies had been named Quadruplet 1, Quadruplet 2, Quadruplet 3 and Quadruplet 4. CP was allowed to bring his camera inside and record the babies. All of us were smiling, laughing, happy. We would not experience this bliss for another decade at least.

Within a few hours, I got my first summons to the NICU. I was encouraged to become physically active after eight and a half months of complete dormancy, and this was when I began going through the strangest of experiences. As long as the babies had been inside me, we had been one unit. Once they came out, I felt bereft. This feeling lasted for at least the first three years of motherhood. Was this postpartum depression? I don't know.

The feeling of sadness and abandonment persisted. The doctors no longer asked me how I felt. The nurses at the NICU were worried about the babies and would constantly badger me. Not a single person came to examine me. No family member enquired about me. Everyone asked only about the babies. The barefoot trudges to the NICU every two hours, repeated urinary infections because of the catheter, a terrible burning sensation all the time, the overwhelming anxiety for Krishna and the laborious feeding of the babies overwhelmed me.

I stopped talking to CP, my parents, my sister and other relatives. This clamp on communication went on to the extent that CP asked me, 'Sangeetha, do you regret the babies?'

The worry and anxiety for Krishna was indescribable. Within two days of his birth, we were told that his renal system had not formed properly and he was not breathing on his own. The girls were drinking ten millilitres of milk every two hours. Krishna was on two drops of milk every two hours, given to him through an ink dropper. I was not allowed to even touch him, but I was taught how to carry the girls securely. Since I had worked with hundreds of newborn puppies, this was no different and I displayed a dexterity that impressed the nurses.

On the sixth day, it was planned that Krishna would be taken off the ventilator. Since I was camping out in the NICU, I got all the inside information by shamelessly eavesdropping when my babies were being discussed. That morning, I strategically positioned myself inside the NICU, but the doctors were having none of it. I was escorted outside and asked to wait, accompanied by a gentle 'Don't worry, we will call you.'

The weaning off the ventilator went smoothly, but Krishna did not put on weight over the next few days.

We were told that the babies would be handed over to us one by one, week by week, to help me get used to taking care of them. The head of the NICU had an exacting protocol for looking after babies. She encouraged me to breastfeed but was compassionate enough to realise that it was tough with four babies. However, I dared not try bottle feeding the babies; it was something she was militantly against. I was taught to patiently feed them formula milk through a tiny contraption called a bondula. Pour milk into the bondula and use it to pour the milk into the waiting mouth of the baby, from the side.

The head of NICU was the warrior goddess for the babies. She kept me on my toes. I demonstrated bundling, unbundling, sponging and cleaning before the first baby was handed over to me at the ward. My eight months' stay at the hospital had created a comfort level in conversing with medical professionals, which would stay with me forever.

The night before we were to receive the first baby, CP got permission for me to accompany him for some shopping. We went to Crawford Market and bought baby mattresses. Red. Blue. Pink. Yellow. Packets and packets of nappies. A ton of white sheets. A ton of napkins. Armfuls of tiny baby clothes.

As CP drove me back to the hospital, my sense of fatigue reached a feverish pitch. I waved bye to him and painfully made my way to the ward. My whole body was burning and consumed by pain. I had never felt so helpless in my life. And then, I got a call from the NICU to feed the babies.

The nurses took one look at me and took me inside a small ante room. They told me that the pain was because I had not fed my babies for more than five hours, and taught me how to express milk. They were so kind to me that I wept.

The next morning was a happy one. Quadruplet 3, Lakshmi, was delivered to me in my cubicle in the general ward. The nurses at the NICU had nicknames for all four babies. Lakshmi had been nicknamed Tomato, for her impressive decibel level and her bright red face. I would leave her with the ayah every two hours and go back to the NICU for the other babies.

Day three saw the entry of Quadruplet 1, Jayashree, nicknamed Butterfly for her delicate looks. With a stuck out lower lip that would wobble when she cried, she was a peaceful baby.

I began to feel the pinch of pressure. Two babies in the ward with me, two in the NICU.

Day five. The nurses at the NICU obviously thought I was ready to cope and handed over Quadruplet 2, Jayanthi. From day one, Jayanthi would snuggle onto my shoulder or sleep with her face down in the pillow and her bum high up in the air, all with a smile on her face and a palpable gentleness. This is what got her the nickname Squirrel.

Our hopes of Quadruplet 4, Krishna, being handed over to us were growing dimmer and dimmer. The first week passed, then the second, third, fourth, fifth, sixth ... we soldiered on. CP would make his granite-faced, back-breaking trips between home in Andheri East, work in Lower Parel, and Bombay Hospital for me. He would see his parents every day, take care of them, see me every day, get me things I needed, take umpteen calls from me on different things related to the babies.

Krishna was finally handed over to us fifty-four days after his birth. There had been fifty-three days of waiting for this boy who had held our entire family in thrall. Fifty-three days of calling the NICU from the general ward intercom at 2.30 in the morning because I knew that was when the nurses began weighing the babies, only to be told, 'No, Sangeetha, he has not put on any weight.' Fifty-three days of shedding silent tears, waiting for my son to grow. Fifty-three days of watching and holding his tiny hands as doctors drew blood for umpteen tests, watching his face grow black with terror as the needle sank in. Fifty-three days of the doctors telling me, 'We've never seen a mother as tough as you.'

We were due to go home the next day. I asked the doctors about scheduling a sterilisation operation to prevent any future pregnancy.

'Just keep your babies alive for two years and show them to us. People go home with two babies and come back with one because something went wrong. You are taking home four underweight babies.'

Before we could take the children home, the NICU doctors called us in for a meeting.

'On your way home, please stop at Dr Parikh's clinic to get a check-up for Krishna's heart, and then Nanavati Hospital for his brain.'

'But,' we protested, 'let us go home together. We will take him to these doctors tomorrow.'

'No' was the inflexible answer. 'He cannot take two journeys. You must do this in a single trip.'

So CP sent our daughters home with a woman colleague, while the two of us escorted Krishna out of Bombay Hospital. We were given an emotional farewell by the matron and nurses of the general ward, the NICU staff, who felt proprietary towards the babies, and even the security guards at the gate.

We left for Dr Parikh's clinic with a dauntingly tiny Krishna. After getting a clean chit, we moved to Nanavati Hospital.

'His brain is fine; he is an Einstein. Don't worry about him.'

With hearts singing with joy and relief, the three of us made our way home.

Amma took the aarti and called us in.

The next tumultuous phase of our life was about to begin.

5
Going home with the babies

From day one of being back home, I looked after my babies and also cooked for everyone—for CP, my in-laws, myself and our two live-in ayahs. What I should have done was send one of the ayahs into the kitchen while I looked after the babies with the other.

Our first ayah entered the Chakrapani Hall of Fame for Helpers by picking up CP's bottles of beer and having a small party with the watchman. The final straw on the camel's back came when, in a fit of temper, she slapped water into Krishna's face while bathing him. He was around eight months old. Krishna was grey and unmoving when Saraswati, the second ayah, brought him to me in the kitchen. I called Dr Philip John, the paediatrician whose clinic was down the lane.

'Bring him right now, you understand? Just run!'

I ran. An auto driver took pity on me, dropped me off and left without taking any money. The nurses waiting for me outside the clinic grabbed Krishna and disappeared without a word. Later that morning, Krishna was admitted to a local hospital for a day. The room was so tiny that I slept below his bed. Nobody asked me if I had eaten anything. I had left home that morning without even a cup of coffee and stayed that way till Krishna was discharged the next day. A grim-faced CP got Lakshmi, the ayah, to pack all her belongings, escorted her to the railway station, stood in a queue himself, managed to procure a ticket for her, got food for her journey, handed over her salary for the entire month and sent her packing.

We were not lucky on this front and had a trail of ayahs traipsing in and out of our home. One of them taught the babies to suck their thumbs so they would sleep. Later, another tried to get them to stop sucking their thumbs by rubbing salt on their fingers. To this day, I wonder if it was the shock of finding salt on her thumb that prevented Jayanthi from forming speech.

The first one and a half years were all about diapers, a house smelling strongly of phenyl, and bedsheets and nappies drying everywhere. Bottles and every utensil used for the babies had to be sterilised, and feeding the babies was a day-long affair. By the time we finished feeding all four, it was time to feed the first baby again! My mother looked anxious. A new Sangeetha seemed to have taken the place of her daughter.

One day, CP wanted me to accompany him to see the new house. He had to ask me three times before I started moving. I just put on my chappals and trailed behind him, looking unkempt. Amma started admonishing me and I came back into my room. Her face brightened because she thought I had decided to freshen up. Instead, I took out a bottle of Relispray, rolled up my salwar, and liberally sprayed it on my legs. Relispray had taken the place of perfume in my life.

I wonder what CP went through those first few years. Neither of us shared our anxiety with the other. I am sure he must have felt overwhelmed with the thought of being the sole provider to a family of six.

My parents-in-law would come home on Sundays to be with the children. My only thought was, 'Will they wake up the babies? I have just got them to sleep.' I would message CP on his mobile: 'Please don't let Amma wake up the children.'

Do I want to take back those words? Yes. Do I want to relive those years as a more joyous mother? Yes, I do.

CP and I realised we had not named the children. My dad, having studied astrology and numerology, produced a long list of names: 'The children are nineteenth born. Every alphabet of the language has a numerical value. The sum total of the name (only the first name) should come to nineteen.'

I waded through the list of names and remembered that Krishna had already been named.

I called Appa.

'I know,' he said calmly. 'Krishna totals nineteen. Don't worry.'

I gave CP the list of names.

He approved.

Quadruplet 1, the youngest, alias Butterfly: Jayashree

Quadruplet 2, alias Squirrel: Devaki (we changed her name to Jayanthi later)

Quadruplet 3, alias Tomato: Lakshmi

Quadruplet 4, the eldest, alias Elephant: Krishna

Whenever I look back, I place myself on a maternal weighing scale. It's an invisible weighing scale that all mothers use to torment themselves needlessly. Did I spend enough time talking to the kids? Did I tell them stories? Did I do justice to each of them? As parents, we keep evaluating ourselves and agonising over the mistakes we made.

I felt unsure of my authority with the live-in ayahs. I looked at my husband like a hungry child looks at a 5 Star chocolate bar that is completely out of reach. I did not have friends to talk to.

I would sing to the babies *all* the time. I would tease them, have imaginary conversations in which I would talk for myself and for them. My father-in-law once said, 'Sangeetha, when they are grown up, your voice will have changed to a singsong one completely.'

The babies were on substitute milk from day one since I was not able to lactate enough. We lined the floor with huge mattresses from one edge of the room to the other so that if they turned or crawled off, nobody would get hurt.

After CP left for work, we would begin bathing the babies. The ayah, Saraswati, taught me to sit with my legs outstretched, place the baby face down lengthwise along my legs, apply oil, flip the baby over and apply oil again, before pouring warm water over the child, holding the baby's nose to ensure water did not go in. I would pass the baby over to be dried and clothed while receiving the second one for bathing. By then, the babies would be ravenously hungry. The ayahs would feed the babies as they emerged from their baths and let them sink into blissful sleep. There would be a two-hour respite, during which the ayahs and I would rest, and I would cook as well.

Anxiety was my twenty-four-hour partner and I looked at the babies as if they were glass dolls. Sometimes we would go down to the parking lot of the building for social interaction. We would spread out a small mat on the floor for Krishna to lie on while the girls toddled around. The helpers in the building and the neighbourhood maalishwali would dole out well-meaning advice that made pangs of inadequacy gnaw at me.

'You don't use "laal tel" to massage him?'

'You don't give him wheatgrass? You must grow it at home and give it to him!'

'Take him to the beach and make him stand in sand.'

Our driver Anil and I went to Juhu beach and brought back a sack of sand. The experiment lasted just two days. It resulted in sand permeating the entire house, and CP giving both Anil and me a piece of his mind.

～

Our first travel with the babies was to get their heads tonsured at Tirupati. We went by train—CP, the babies, one ayah and I. I quickly swept our compartment clean with a small broom that I had carried with me for that purpose. I slept on the floor between the two lower berths. It turned out to be a wise decision.

No sooner had the train started to move, all four babies tumbled towards me and sprawled across my lap.

After the tonsuring, we went to Chennai for the 'ayush homam', invoking the grace of the gods and the blessings of elders for the children.

There is something reassuringly anonymous about one-year-old babies. Except for the fact that Krishna was not yet walking, the babies were seen, praised, cuddled and smothered with affection, with no questions asked. In the years to come, sympathy, worry, alarm and horror were to get finely enmeshed with the reactions that these babies would evoke. Right then, all of them were cute, sweet, huggable and lovable.

Krishna had a very difficult time as an infant and child. Because he had weighed only 940 grams at birth, his muscle tone was poor, and it was only through relentless physiotherapy and his own determination that he finally walked at the age of three. Worse, his renal system was malformed, which demanded a series of reconstructive surgeries. The first surgery was to take place after our return from Chennai.

We had been looking forward to this eagerly and had made several recce trips between the doctors' clinics and the hospital.

On the day of the surgery, I wore a brand-new yellow saree that CP had brought me from Calcutta, unworried, heart dancing with anticipation.

Oh, how foolish I was!

Halfway through the operation, the surgeon called us in and drew a diagram on a piece of paper, explaining why the surgery would have to be postponed for a few weeks. All I knew was that our chance of happiness with Krishna was gone. Over the next two years, until we met Dr Amdekar who was able to convince us to wait ten years so Krishna was old enough, nine more surgical interventions were carried out and none of them worked. We had to maintain a sterile environment at home for Krishna's sake. With four babies in a small flat, it was no easy task.

Between the ages of one and a half and two years, there were rapid changes in the children. Krishna started crawling! To see him determinedly racing on all fours after his sisters was a joy. However, he could not sit or walk yet. We were recommended a chair that would keep him upright with his chest, abdomen, thighs and legs strapped so he would be forced to assume a sitting position.

That morning was a dismal one. The chair-maker came home and insisted on showing me a picture album of the chair being used by various children and adults. I was both saddened and terrified of what the future held. I paid him a deposit of Rs 2,500 and asked him to try and get it made before our trip to Chennai ten days later. He said it would take at least a month.

Our trip to Chennai was filled with anxiety. The children had crossed the magic age of one. We knew and the world knew that the children were not like other thriving babies. Jayanthi had not started babbling, much less saying even a single word. Krishna was wrinkled and tired, holding up a weary body under a huge head with bright, inquisitive eyes. Lakshmi had 'Amma' for me and 'Allo' for the 'Hello' she would say into her toy phone. Jayashree became close buddies with Lakshmi and would be up to some mischief or the other with her all the time.

By the time we got back to Mumbai, Krishna had managed to hold his body up in a sitting position. The physiotherapist told us that Krishna would no longer need the chair. I called the chair-maker home, paid him the balance Rs 6,000, and told him to use it for a needy child who could not afford it. I placed the cheque against the large and timeworn picture of Lord Balaji in our living room and prayed that this chair should keep being passed around and never be needed permanently by anyone.

But the issues were far from over. Krishna could not come to standing position, leave alone walk. Several surgeries were done one after another with no solution emerging. When I came back after ten days of hospitalisation with Krishna, the house looked the same, but the children had changed.

6
How could I be depressed?

I WEIGHED FIFTY-SIX KILOS WHEN I WAS DISCHARGED AFTER delivery. In the two years that followed, I had put on nine kilos. By the time the kids turned ten, I weighed seventy-four kilos, and today, I weigh ninety-four. Food had become my secret lover. It was during a chance conversation with Saadiyah Merchant, a senior occupational therapist, that I realised what had happened. The conversation went thus:

'Parents go through a lot of anxiety, Sangeetha. Counselling helps.'

'Saadiyah, what about the time a child is diagnosed? Does the parent have a likelihood of going into depression?'

'Yes, Sangeetha, there are many signs of depression. Even overeating is a sign.'

I did not let her continue.

'Overeating, Saadiyah?'

'Oh yes, even overeating is a sign of depression.'

To this day, I can't accept that I am depressed. I am a strong person, I have faced challenges head on, I have reinvented my relationship with my husband and brought him down from the out-of-reach 5 Star chocolate bar to the Jai–Veeru camaraderie of

Sholay fame. I've said goodbye to being a contented stay-at-home mother and become a woman who runs an organisation, designs teaching programmes, and provides services to families with autism. How can I be depressed?

When I returned with Krishna after being with him at the hospital for ten days, the first thing I did was run into the children's room. I could run in those days. The room was half-bathed in early morning sunlight. Lakshmi and Jayanthi were sleeping. Jayashree was awake. I rushed towards her. She looked at me curiously and turned towards Sarita, the ayah, seeking approval. Sarita nodded, and Jayashree got up and toddled towards me.

Even after so many years, the memory hurts. Of course, I had laughed it off then.

Whacking her playfully, I had said, 'You want permission to come to Amma?'

By then, Jayanthi was awake. I brought their porridge out and sat down with four bowls. We all sat on the floor since the chairs had been shunted into CP's room.

I called Jayanthi who was sitting a few inches away from me. In those days, her name was Devaki.

'Devaki, come.

'Devaki.

'Devaki.'

It was eerie. She was only a few inches away from me. She did not even turn to look at me.

I shouted.

No response.

Finally, I physically turned her around. She ate quietly.

As the day progressed, I saw her picking up a small toy and holding it right in front of her eyes as if she was trying to look through it. Lakshmi had not progressed beyond uttering 'Amma' and 'Allo'. We could see her going further and further away from the world Jayashree and Krishna inhabited.

We reassured ourselves with other mitigating achievements, such as Lakshmi standing in front of the TV and imitating nursery rhymes effortlessly. CP and I carried umbrellas of hope to shield us from the steady pitter patter of rainfall, but as time passed, we looked down and saw the land slide under our feet.

This was when CP decided that enough was enough. Jayanthi had already moved away from us and Lakshmi was getting markedly slower in her responses and interaction by the day. Krishna spent more time in hospital than at home and that left poor, valiant Jayashree holding up the quadruplet structure.

CP cautiously and determinedly approached me.

'I have found out about a doctor. Dr Y.K. Amdekar.'

'CP, nobody will be able to understand Krishna's complexity of problems. In any case, we are already struggling.'

'Sangeetha, we need help. I have heard so much about Dr Amdekar. Come and meet him.'

We were batting at subzero. Doctor visits, hospital visits, clinical consultations, coming back home with empty hearts and tired souls. The only security I had were the people who had known us from the time the babies were born. I reluctantly agreed to meet Dr Amdekar.

After meeting him for the first time, I wept. Somebody had finally listened to us, allowed us to explain our anxieties and, taking a piece of paper and pencil, told us what to do and what to expect. More importantly, he told us what he could do for us.

CP is a man of foresight, I have always believed that. But by having the courage to step out of a comfort zone and walking to the doorstep of Dr Amdekar, he changed the collective fortunes of the Chakrapani family.

Dr Amdekar referred us to the surgeon Dr Subhash Dalal. We met him late at night in his Pedder Road clinic. Dr Dalal looked at the child in our arms and told us that we would have to accept a stopgap solution to Krishna's problem. He patted CP on the shoulder and refused a consultation fee.

This grave man, my husband, standing by my side, responded to the silent empathy and bent down to touch the surgeon's feet.

We left and stood outside the building, unsure of what the future held, but backed by the indomitable Dr Amdekar.

The stopgap surgery was done and Krishna didn't have to go back to the hospital for ten years. Dr Amdekar was unmoved and unperturbed by my periodic visits to his clinic, asking for Krishna's surgeries to be done. He made me wait for ten years before allowing Krishna to be touched, allowing the child precious time to grow.

We also took Jayanthi to Dr Amdekar. 'She is not responding to her name.'

He listened to us carefully and referred us to Dr Vibha Krishnamurthy, a developmental paediatrician and founder of Ummeed Child Development Centre. The evening before our appointment, I had several imaginary conversations with Dr Vibha, mentally conjuring up a saree-clad lady with an impeccably coiffed bun. I recorded Jayanthi smiling at her toys, imitating the actions of nursery rhymes and smiling at her siblings.

As we waited at reception, there was no sign of the saree-clad figure I was looking for. The receptionist asked us to follow a young, slightly built person who I had assumed was a college student. With a gentle smile, the person motioned to us to follow her. I was taken aback when I realised that this was Dr Vibha.

The doctor proceeded to lightly sit on the floor in a small room. She gently chatted and interacted with Jayanthi for the next hour or maybe longer. She looked up at us.

'Jayanthi shows signs of autism,' Dr Vibha said.

Everything else she said washed away and away and away.

CP and I, beleaguered by our journey over the last three years, had become strangers to one another.

We were bound by our duty, responsibility and love for our children, but infinitely wary of each other. As we sat at Ummeed Child Development Centre's reception to be given Dr Vibha's report after she had met Jayanthi, I kept waiting for CP to talk to me. To say what he felt. To ask how I felt. But there was nothing.

Did I reach out? Did I ask for support? Did I ask him what he was thinking? No!

I wish we could have stayed back at Ummeed that day. I wish we had spent the whole day with Dr Vibha. I wish she had had a magic telescope that would let us peek at the many-splendoured and also the multiple frustrating aspects of autism.

We bid a civil goodbye to Dr Vibha and, clutching her report, got into the car. I opened the file.

'Autism is a lifelong developmental disability and …'

I did not read further.

I wallowed in misery but started consulting an occupational therapist. I watched in amazement as the therapist broke up tasks and Jayanthi successfully played a series of games with her. The same Jayanthi who would not engage with me in a single activity.

Method had to become our god in reaching out to Jayanthi. The therapist suggested working on her oral motor skills by rubbing a variety of textures and tastes on her gums: lemon juice, honey, etc. This had to be done three times a day. We also hoisted her up by her feet and made her walk around the house on her hands to stimulate her vestibular system. Because Jayanthi had not formed teeth, I started making her chomp down on soft pieces of chapati. Within weeks, her teeth sprouted. However, she still could not chew and could not be given solid foods.

From a mother, I became a manager. I tried to run the home efficiently while dispensing equal attention—mind you, not equal affection—to the children. There was no time for affection.

Being different has many textures. Celebrities, entrepreneurs and athletes have reaped the rewards for being different: a cut above the rest.

Neurodivergence is about being a cut *away* from the rest. It's about struggling to keep up. It's about trying out different masks, hoping that at least one of them helps you merge with the crowd. It's about parents swaying and curving and turning themselves inside out to make their children with autism—who look just like others but are not at all like others—fit with the others.

This goes on till the parents realise that autism is a different kind of life to be lived. It's like the pieces of broken glass that come together to finally create a stained-glass window. It takes time for the parents and the world to appreciate the many textures of this person with autism who is made of broken glass, pieces that reach and impact every nook and corner of their personality. Yes, they may not comprehend many things, may not travel the journey of a regular person, may struggle and need support, but all together, seen as a person, this individual with autism is a unique and beautiful stained-glass window that needs some care and support to achieve and live their best life.

I did not know this then. I did not know that I needed time to understand and appreciate my children with autism.

It was at this point that Anahita Nariman, speech therapist, entered our lives. Speech therapy, I discovered, is not only about forming speech in your children, but a style of working with enthusiasm, throwing the voice, singing, making sounds, and breaking the wall of reserve between you and your child. I observed her and absorbed like a sponge.

Anahita would sing to Lakshmi. She even recorded songs for her. Not only would Lakshmi listen to these songs keenly, she would even try to join in. One evening, we finished a session and got into the car at 7 p.m. It would take us two hours to get home. I had a pack of chocolate cookies with me.

'Break up a cookie into tiny pieces. Lakshmi is now able to say "biscuit". Don't give her even one piece until she asks for it,' the therapist's words rang in my ears.

For the next two hours, Lakshmi and I wrangled over the cookies.

It worked. She asked for a cookie.

One morning, Lakshmi was sitting in the kitchen with me. Like M.S. Subbulakshmi's *Suprabhatam*, Anahita's voice was being played. Just as Anahita had advised, I paused the recording abruptly. Hesitantly, Lakshmi sang the rest of the words.

We tried this with Jayanthi too, but it did not work. One of the overriding reasons was that Jayanthi did not want anything. Food, water, juice, toys—zilch. She was content within herself so there was no room for negotiation.

But Anahita set Jayanthi free from the shackles of pureed food by helping me learn how to teach Jayanthi to chew and eat. For days, weeks and months on end, I would sit with Jayanthi with differently textured food, break it into small pieces, keep a piece between her teeth, and manually move her jaws up and down till the food was smashed and swallowed. To this day, Jayanthi uses her finger to push hard food between her teeth and chomp down on it. And she has mastered a set of mysterious actions for eating soft foods.

The school-going period of our lives had begun.

I found a sweet and homely playschool in our area. The school was a success for everyone except Jayanthi. She could not follow instructions the way the others could. She was not toilet-trained and had to be diapered. She had zero communication and needed the complete, undivided attention of one person at the school.

The children were now nearly three years old. We shifted to our new home—CP's dream home, into which he had sunk his savings while I lay pregnant in hospital. The new home that CP had personally designed, ensuring there was a terrace. The new home that would realise the dream of a young CP who had grown up in a chawl and then gone on to become a grave man with multiple responsibilities ahead of him.

Despite the hidden rancour between CP and me, something Himalayan lay at the bottom layer of our relationship, which has helped us survive. That morning, as I got the babies ready to move into our new home, someone known to me told me terrible things that apparently CP thought of me—about us being a complete failure. I don't know from where the steel emerged in my mind. I don't know how and from where faith remained in me for myself, my children and my husband, how I pinned that faith to my chest and walked erect. What did I have as armour against the cruel darts that pierced my delicate skin that day? It was the commitment we both had already demonstrated towards our children, akin to twenty years within two years. It was the relentless planning that I have seen CP do to secure the future of his fragile and needy family, and it was my infinite faith in our combined strength to face the future.

I had a wooden toy set with five different shapes in five different colours. CP was trying to look busy as I invited Lakshmi to complete the activity with me. She could not. My heart thudded so loudly that I wondered how CP did not hear it. Again and again, I tried. She would not look at me. The next morning, we were in Dr Amdekar's clinic. He asked us to meet Dr Vibha again. We refused.

CP asked Dr Amdekar again and again, 'Shall I show you how she understands everything, doctor? All I need to do is frown and she starts crying. A small smile and she laughs and laughs. Wait, I will ask her to sing a nursery rhyme for you.'

Dr Amdekar listened and then asked us to meet Dr Vibha.

Dr Vibha is seared into my soul. She lives within me. Her voice is as familiar to me as the cocklebells in Lakshmi's laughter, the gurgle in Jayanthi's throat, the infectious chuckles of Krishna and the flute-like sweetness of Jayashree's voice. Dr Vibha's voice is the fifth one in my heart, and as long as I live, it will be with me. Her words, 'It is autism', her expression, her calm demeanour, what she was wearing that day, the shapes she drew on paper for Lakshmi to copy are welded onto my soul. Neither CP nor I had anything to say to each other this time, but we could not go home. CP took us to Mahalakshmi temple. Prayer was the last thing on our minds, but we could not think of a better refuge at that point in time.

We wandered around the temple, closely watching Lakshmi whose future was now tainted. By the time we reached home, it was past midnight. Lakshmi slept. CP sat by her side and wept like a baby.

From that day onward, our home became a railway station with multiple tracks. The children boarded different trains, the arrival and departure timings differed, and CP and I began live auditioning for the roles of engine driver and conductor respectively.

CP and I promoted Dr Vibha from Gabbar Singh to Thakur of *Sholay* fame and knocked at her door again. She gave us refuge at Ummeed for three months—admission for Jayashree and Krishna in the playschool on their premises, and the mother and child autism programme for Lakshmi, Jayanthi and me. Three months of wearing a snorkel mask, going underwater and discovering the myriad colours of autism. There were two parts of me functioning simultaneously from that day onward: the mother who was looking for the complete transformation of her children, and a novice being trained in autism.

While there are many things that are unexplained about autism, parents will testify with world-weary eyes that there are no alternatives to therapy and working with the child at home. Daily living skills. Speech therapy. Occupational therapy. Language and communication. Behaviour modification. Sensory integration. Academic intervention. The years and years of help, therapy and professional inputs are frustratingly small building blocks that pave the way for an empowered future—a future when the magical period of childhood ends, the journey to adulthood begins, and one has to start making the best of what one has acquired.

We started exploring school options during this three-month period at Ummeed. We admitted the children into an inclusive school: Jayashree and Krishna in Higher KG, and Lakshmi and Jayanthi in Lower KG.

On the first day, I wore a dark green short kurta. It was the first time I was wearing a short kurta. It had started raining heavily. I took them by car and unlike the other children, mine did not even whimper, much less cry, on being separated from me. They were too busy managing themselves. I handed them over one by one. Krishna was carried into the school. He had not begun walking yet, and was undergoing intense physiotherapy every alternate day. He wasn't showing any improvement, and we were getting tired of rushing here and there.

Those initial days of the children going to school were heady. Only an autism parent will understand the joy of buying a school uniform, school bag and lunchbox, organising an identity card, waving bye to their child with autism as they blessedly merge with a crowd of beautiful neurotypical children.

This joyful period lasted for around two years till they hit Class II. Not that it was smooth sailing entirely till then. Jayanthi got a pureed banana for the short break and pureed idli with tomato soup for lunch. Her teeth and tongue were dormant. Not only did she not have speech, she also did not have communication. None of us knew Jayanthi—what she liked, what she wanted, who she was.

I was so happy that my four children were going to school that it slipped my mind that they had to study. I was so grateful for the school accepting Lakshmi and Jayanthi lovingly that it slipped my mind that Jayashree and Krishna, in Class II, were not up to the mark. One evening, I received a call from the school. 'Please check the diaries in Jayashree and Krishna's bags.'

Diaries? Four years since they had joined school and I did not know that they had diaries in which teachers wrote notes! There were pages and pages of notes. Homework not completed. Untidy work. Pencil box not carried. Notebooks left at home.

Holding the diaries, I thought, 'What kind of a mother am I?'

I had to learn how to wear two pairs of shoes simultaneously. I had to learn to walk two different tracks, speak two different languages—one with few words, the other with a rich vocabulary. I had to tell two different kinds of stories—one with actions and pictures, the other complex and challenging.

∼

A few months after we moved to our new home, we went to Khandala for a short holiday. We stayed in an HDFC Bank guest house that belonged to the Zaveri family. It was a huge house with an open kitchen where twenty people could cook simultaneously.

CP had to go back to Mumbai the same day for some urgent work. He said he would return the same evening.

By five in the evening, the babies, Jaya the caregiver, and I were restless in the big, dark, old guest house. 'Let's go for a walk,' I said.

Arming ourselves with umbrellas, Jaya and I put the children into raincoats. Jaya held two by their hands. I held one by the hand and carried Krishna. The watchman suggested going to the Ganpati temple in the next lane. Halfway down the path, I put Krishna down and tried to encourage him to walk while holding my hand. He could not.

Angry, sad and frustrated, I picked him up and we continued walking. We reached the temple and heard the rush of a vehicle behind us. It was CP. He had returned to the guest house and the watchman had guided him to us. We entered the small and quiet temple. The Elephant God looked on quietly as we went around the pradakshina.

'Krishna, tell him that the next time you come to this temple, you will come walking,' I told my baby.

Late in the evening, two days after we returned to Mumbai from Khandala, Jaya was playing with the girls as Krishna leaned upright against my legs. For an infinitesimal second, he let go and then caught me again. My breath stopped. I gently pushed him a wee bit away and let go. His eyes widened in alarm, but he placed his foot forward and caught me. I pushed him a little further and let go. He wobbled two steps and reached me. He started laughing and screaming with excitement.

Jaya and the girls turned to see what was going on. I asked Jaya to stand against the wall at the other end of the room and pushed Krishna. He ran non-stop, shouting with laughter, till he bumped against Jaya. She pushed him back towards me. He ran with amazement writ large on his face. We did this ten times before I called Dr Madhavi, the physiotherapist.

'Doctor, he is moving from one point to another on his own, without support. Is this not called walking?'

'Yes, Sangeetha.'

'Are you sure? I want to tell CP, but what if he stops walking before CP gets home?'

'No, that will not happen. You can tell him.'

'But, doctor, he is not able to stop once he starts walking.'

'We will have to wait and see. Physio will continue.'

I took Krishna to the puja room, made him do 'namaskar', and then called CP.

CP did not express his ecstasy like I did. Maybe years of anxiety and disappointments had hardened him.

⁓

I was not ready to accept how different a person CP is from me. I felt resentful and lonely. Today, I value him and his immense role as a father. Yes, the children still talk about him being a reserved father, one you would think twice about before approaching. He would take them on outings and long car rides, but the channel of communication between them was strained. Today, they have grown up and appreciate their multidimensional father. I have spent many evenings telling them about his chequered childhood and how the travails of the past influence our present. They agreed with me that while he does not wax poetic or say dreamy things like, 'Name it, you will have it', he is acutely responsible and has paved their paths with undeniable security.

Today, I value myself as an individual. I like the fact that I say things and feel things and do things, both practical and imaginative. I remember a saying that I chanced upon many years ago: 'If I love you, what business is it of yours?' I have learnt to value CP and myself as two unique and independent individuals and not piggyback my feelings onto his.

⁓

Toilet training is a minefield in the lives of children with autism and their parents. Despite the training from the time the babies started walking, Lakshmi and Jayanthi had not responded. Jayanthi had to be taken to the toilet at regular intervals for her small job. She would do her big job in her underwear and sit in a fixed posture—a signal that I had to clean her up. Naturally, even our helpers found the task distasteful.

Lakshmi's monstrous habit of relieving herself all over the house had to be stopped, but try as I might, she refused to use the toilet for her big job. We went for a holiday to my sister Vaidehi's place. Vaidehi's own baby, Sneha, was a wee toddler then. Freed from the compulsions of running a home, I bought suppositories from the medical shop. The ayah who was travelling with me kept an eye on the rest of the kids. I took Lakshmi inside one of the rooms after her lunch and started playing with her. At some point, she began the war dance that was a precursor to doing her big job. I picked her up, placed her on my lap and inserted a suppository in the anus. Just three years old, she looked at me indignantly and jumped off. Those days, I was thirty kilos lighter and caught her. Then I placed her strategically in the toilet.

When she did her big job in the toilet, the expression of amazement on her face was priceless. Oh! This is so simple. Nevertheless, we played 'suppository, suppository' twice more before Lakshmi abandoned the war dance and shifted to more civilised habits. These battles were fought, sometimes lost and sometimes won, on a daily basis.

7
Stumbling towards childhood

As the four children stumbled from toddlerhood to childhood, CP and I grew more and more distant.

I vividly remember a conversation with Sister Melba Rodrigues. She had been the principal of Jesus and Mary College, Delhi University, where I had studied between 1991 and 1993. Her majestic aura of dignity, wisdom and spirituality drew me to her and has kept our friendship thriving even after so many years.

It was 2008. I had brought the children to a relatively uncrowded park near my home. I stood at the fringe of the park and called Sister.

'Sister, I just want to run away. I can't deal with this.'

Sister listened. 'I will pray for you and your family, Sangeetha. You know you will face this challenge.'

Imagine how CP could have felt! He too must have dreamed of a pretty wife, a child, raising a family together and living in harmony with his parents. Poof! He did not get any of his wishes. We haven't talked about this, but when I relive my misery of those years, I can't help but feel sad for his demolished dreams.

The school was kind about Lakshmi and Jayanthi's limited accomplishments, but their smiles faded and their concerns grew as the children inched into Class II.

It did not strike me that Lakshmi and Jayanthi were not flourishing in the school environment anymore. Their peers were reading stories, vying to be class monitors, selecting birthday outfits and writing exams. Lakshmi and Jayanthi were working on alphabet recognition and pattern writing. Lakshmi was removing her shirt regularly in class, Jayanthi was soiling her uniform and causing unpleasantness for everybody. Lakshmi had started hitting the teachers and children in her class, Jayanthi did not know how to ask for food. If the school didi forgot to give her the lunchbox, she would sit quietly in a classroom full of children who were eating their lunch.

I could have:

1. Given them better academic support to supplement what was being taught to them at school.
2. Understood that their potential lay elsewhere and allowed them to learn pre-vocational skills while continuing to develop reading and writing skills.
3. If I had had the bigness of vision and depth of understanding back then, I would have given Lakshmi and Jayanthi the fresh air of acceptance that they were gasping for.

But, no! I was not ready. The words 'special school' were like a thousand spiders climbing up my back.

When the children were young, I was more taskmaster and less mother as I danced the dance of behaviour modification and devised techniques to teach daily living skills. Life skills for someone with autism can range from brushing teeth to learning to use the health faucet to keep the bum clean to not taking off clothes in public to eating independently ... the list goes on.

Another reality is that life is not a vipassana course. Silence and life are two contrasting realities. From the moment we are born till the moment we die, language and communication support the existence of life. For people with autism, vipassana is a way of life, and language and communication are foreign sciences that have to be learnt so they can coexist with others.

Often the skin of our inner thighs becomes scratchy and irritable because of perspiration. Some years ago, I saw Jayanthi walking remarkably like a penguin. She was around seven years old then. I went with her to the bathroom and asked her to roll down her pants while keeping her innerwear on. Both her inner thighs were red. She looked down and then at me with big eyes. I said, 'Wait.'

I brought Vaseline and made her take some with her fingers. Then, placing my hand over her hand, I got her to apply it all over the affected area. From then on, I have ensured that Vaseline is available in all the bathrooms. Even now, Jayanthi is not fully independent. She comes to me and points towards her inner thighs to show me that they hurt. I open the Vaseline container and stand outside the bathroom while she helps herself.

Lakshmi and Jayanthi use very limited speech. In fact, many people with autism are not easy to understand when they speak. Lakshmi has code words: 'Papi' for French fries, 'order' for ordering food from outside, 'raita' for eating out at a hotel and 'kaja' for Shah Rukh Khan songs. Lakshmi does not like to talk except when she must. She loves to sing, hates to ask for help and stubbornly tries to do everything herself. When she is not well and sometimes throws up her food, Lakshmi insists on cleaning up. So imagine her frustration if she is not able to articulate what she wants, particularly regarding food!

This is where communication devices come to the help of people with autism. Lakshmi uses an AAC (alternative and augmentative communication) book that has a pictorial menu card to help her choose her food. In fact, the AAC book helps a person with autism to use pictures to communicate from dawn to dusk.

Jayanthi was non-verbal except for when she was around two years old. She would babble, 'Dha dha dha.' Then she stopped that too. By the time she was around four years old, she and I needed help to communicate with each other.

There followed a long period of silence. Jayanthi kept to herself till around the age of six. Then she started expressing herself by pointing to things she wanted. Basic functional signs. Touching feet for shoes, hair for comb, mouth for food.

Jayanthi and I joined a sign language school. After a couple of weeks I realised that Indian sign language is not suited for people with autism. It is too complex and not functional. So I made a book of simple signs and started using it with Jayanthi.

It was a war of sorts to understand each other. There is a part of parenting that requires no understanding. It is effortless. It occurs when a mother hugs her child and both sleep peacefully in the darkness of the night. It occurs when you can't even see each other's faces, when just the touch of the mother is enough for a whoosh of comfort to settle in the heart of the child. However, when daylight dawns, the child struggles to understand what is expected of them while the parent grows increasingly exhausted trying to understand what the child wants. This struggle between what the child with autism wants and what is expected of them is long, and it stretches across home, school and social situations.

When Jayanthi turned eighteen, CP approached me. 'Sangeetha, don't give up,' he said. 'Try for speech again.'

I called up Anahita Nariman and threatened to shift from Andheri East, where I lived, to Colaba, where she lives, if she couldn't come to us. She promised to try and help Jayanthi, though any hope for speech at such a late age was dim.

For two years, Anahita and Jayanthi went on a gritty journey, learning to make sounds, manipulate the tongue, string the sounds together to make words.

Jayanthi now says 'Amma' and looks at me in wonderment because she can say something. She can say about thirty words, though her pronunciation is extremely obscure. She holds her nose between her thumb and index finger to produce the sound of 'b' for bye. She blows into a flute while holding her nose tightly to help her push air out from her mouth. She has discovered that a tongue exists in her mouth and carols 'la la la la' when she wants to sing. For everything else, she signs.

Our lives are all about finding anything that works.

Around 2007, when the children were about four years old, a chance conversation with a neighbour, Gomathi Mami, brought Sai Baba into my life. By then, I had a book full of prayers. I had an ongoing research project on who among the pantheon of gods and goddesses was most likely to answer my prayers. However, my anxiety for my children had converted me from a believer to negotiator, from experiencing the divine to making demands and chanting prayers feverishly. I had to find god all over again.

In our bid to erase autism from our lives, we had tried homeopathy through at least three practitioners, apart from acupressure, acupuncture and IVIG (intravenous immunoglobulin). We had visited pundits and sages, temples, churches and mosques. We had consulted astrologers, face readers, palmists, mystics and men of religion. We had changed Devaki's name to Jayanthi because we were told the letter 'J' is a lucky initial, bringing great success to those whose names begin with it.

One evening, as I sat at a neighbour's home reading the *Sri Sai Satcharitra*, something happened that marked the start of a series of remarkable experiences. A beautiful white etching of Lord Krishna appeared on the windowpane in front of me: a young Krishna wearing a long, flared tunic, feet crossed, flute at his lips and peacock feather tucked in the crown of his head. I tried in vain to show the etching to the others, but nobody else could see it.

A few months later, I dreamt that Sathya Sai Baba had entered the kitchen and started cleaning the dirty platform that was littered with leftover food. In my dream, I pleaded with Baba to stop. Not taking my eyes off his face, I walked backwards to CP's room, quickly brought out a new dhoti, spread it on a chair and made Baba sit down. After I woke up, I went to the kitchen and stared at the mess I had left it in. I cleared everything up. Never again, I vowed to myself, will I leave an unpleasant work area for someone else to clean up.

That evening, CP bought a chair and a permanent seating place was installed for Sai Baba at the altar.

I would wake up early in the morning to say my prayers. When I went for my bath and locked the bathroom door, I would hear someone with bells on their feet running up and down outside. The sounds were loud. Unmistakable. By the time I hastily dressed and came out, there would be nobody there.

Devotees started gifting Sai Baba pictures to us, and the altar became bigger and bigger. Early one morning, I draped a garland on Shirdi Sai Baba's idol. It slipped and fell off. I laughed and told him, 'Your garland has fallen off.' The next instant, the garland rose and draped itself around him again.

CP silently watched my intense journey of faith with Sai Baba and restricted himself to saying, 'Give others a chance to worship him. Leave him be for some time.'

On the sacred day of Pongal, I made both venn pongal (with salt and pepper) and chakkara pongal (with jaggery) and offered it to Baba. Shortly afterwards, I served breakfast to CP.

'There is no salt in the venn pongal,' he said.

I went into the kitchen, took some salt and lightly sprinkled it over the venn pongal in front of Baba's altar. 'I am not mixing it,' I told him. 'Anyway, you never eat what I give you.'

The next morning when I went to say my prayers, there were pieces of rock salt scattered all around his altar.

I soaked myself in the sunshine of my discovery of Baba. I immersed myself in books written by his devotees on their sturdy journeys of faith, devoid of miracle cures. It took me years to realise and understand that he had come to help me forge a path of acceptance and form a vision to help my children, other children, my family and other families.

~

Jayashree was a very obedient child; painfully so. She hovered over Lakshmi and Jayanthi all the time. During break time at school, she would leave her classroom and go to the Higher KG classroom where Lakshmi and Jayanthi were, to make sure they were alright.

Jayashree never told me about this daily routine of hers. It was her class teacher who asked me, 'Mrs Chakrapani, have you asked Jayashree to take care of Lakshmi and Jayanthi during break?'

I was stupefied. My heart became small with misery when I thought of the silent anxiety that Jayashree was feeling for her vulnerable sisters. I was so preoccupied that I did not tell the teachers about Krishna's medical condition. Krishna was in the school for about seven years, up to Class VI. Would anyone believe this glaring omission on a mother's part? Krishna never said a word about it to his friends or teachers. When we had our last parent–teacher meeting before leaving the school, I talked about Krishna with his class teacher and she was stunned. I felt miserable. How could I have been so remiss?

Do all parents of children with special needs swing back and forth like a yo-yo? Being too involved with their children with special needs and not giving enough attention to their neurotypical children? Focusing too much on their neurotypical children and not working hard on those with special needs? Do they feel guilty? Do they revisit the earlier years and wish they had done X instead of Y? Yes!

Do these parents need friends? Do they need someone to talk to? Yes!

Do they experience more marital issues than the average couple? Do they need support from their extended families? Yes, most definitely.

Are there financial challenges? Do parents need to keep shelling out money way beyond the adult years of their children with special needs, for medical care, vocational training, rehabilitation and lifetime care? Yes!

I tried to navigate this maze. I forced myself to write down the goals we had for our family and what Lakshmi and Jayanthi needed the most. All of a sudden, life at home was running on six to seven tracks at a time. Jayashree and Krishna were admitted into a new school. Putting away Lakshmi and Jayanthi's school uniforms was a nightmare. Seeing Jayashree and Krishna leave for school without Lakshmi and Jayanthi was incredibly painful.

8
Growing up ... together

WHEN LAKSHMI GOT HER FIRST PERIOD, I WAS AT THE LOCAL grocery store. The helper called me. 'Lakshmi's clothes are stained. She has become a big girl.'

I hastily told her, 'You know the steps. Help her get changed.' Then, I rushed home.

Lakshmi was sitting in front of the computer, playing games. I went to her. She turned and, for an instant that I can never ever forget, broke into tears against me and cried, 'Amma.'

I cried too, as we both realised that something had changed forever.

It took three months for Lakshmi to master the steps of changing her sanitary napkins, six months to learn the rules of cleanliness, and even now, after seven years, I do surprise checks to ensure that she is keeping herself and the bathroom clean.

Can I take this liberty with a seventeen-year-old neurotypical teenager? Most definitely not. Will a verbal revision with Lakshmi be enough? Again, no! So I talk to her and explain that I want to help, and stand outside the washroom with the door slightly ajar as I instruct her to use the jet spray and clean herself thoroughly. Balancing health and hygiene for a child with autism while respecting their privacy is a tightrope walk that parents and caregivers must navigate throughout life.

When Jayanthi started her period, it was like explaining the reproductive system to Bambi the deer. She took much longer than Lakshmi, but what really came in the way and still does is her other-worldly aura. Imagine a daffodil or a lily going through the menstrual cycle—so incongruous and so cruel. While these feelings raged within me, I wore the mask of a Sam Manekshaw and taught the regimen day in and day out, day in and day out.

As the kids touched eleven, Dr Amdekar finally agreed to plan the series of delicate surgeries that would reshape Krishna's renal system.

CP was wracked with anxiety. He worried Krishna would suffer once again. The night before the surgery, he visited Krishna and me at the hospital.

'Call it off, Sangeetha,' he said.

'No, CP, he will be fine,' I responded.

'Mark my words, if something goes wrong, you will never be able to forgive yourself,' he said and stalked to the elevator.

Over the next four months, Krishna underwent four surgeries. CP watched over him like a hawk. He would go back and forth to work. I stayed at the hospital with Krishna, running the house remotely with the aid of helpers. After the last surgery was successfully completed, the three of us returned home, more relieved than triumphant.

～

People were fooled by the plastic smile I had on my face. CP and I were two strangers under one roof and would speak with feverish intensity only when it came to the children. I was so alone that I could have screamed, I could have wept.

CP and I had a tumultuous relationship. Our different personalities. Our rough and tumble introduction to parenthood.

Just the nine months to delivery took the greatest toll on CP. I at least had the babies inside me. He was alone.

In the Margazhi stories in this book, you'll see the happy, sad and difficult sides to our relationship. There are three reasons for this.

One, as the children grew older and inched their way towards the age of ten, there came a big turning point in our relationship. Between all of us. Not only between CP and me, but even with the children. The children started bonding with us. Asking questions.

Two, I accepted myself. I came into my own. I no longer saw myself through CP's eyes. I stopped judging myself by our relationship. I learnt to value him and develop a bond with him without the 'husband' tag and the millions of expectations that come along with it. I began to love my children and not see them as only problems to be solved. I stopped looking for cures for autism. We continued to be beset with problems and issues on all sides—medical, developmental, educational, parental. No one day was ever like another.

And three, my sense of humour asserted itself. In 2011, I started writing Margazhi stories. The children were nine. I would wake up at approximately three in the morning, bathe, light the lamps, draw a rangoli, take a photo, and then sit to write. My mind would wander and I would remember some episode. As I wrote, the humour began to assert itself. Sometimes, the pain would assert itself.

I can never plan and write. I can never think, this is what I am going to write. I start writing and then my thoughts merge together and something is expressed. When I started writing the Margazhi stories, I found that beneath all the tumult, we were—and are—a very strong family.

Despite all the hurdles, we have stuck by each other and never given up.

The Margazhi stories found a lot of love among readers. At home, they have been healing. The children and CP would read my stories and there was the same dawning realisation in them too.

But at that time, after Krishna's final surgeries, I pondered and pondered over my complex relationship with CP and gave it another name—friendship. That really set me free. I was free of expectations and stopped evaluating everything in our home. The children began to realise that they could not expect their parents to smile at each other continuously. Similarly, I set myself free and stopped judging myself as a life partner. I began to like myself.

Play is one of the most fundamental parts of childhood, and its importance does not decrease even when we become adults. Across the lifespan of an adult, play ranges from hide and seek to ludo to cricket to competitive sport to reading, painting, games on the computer and watching movies. Essentially, play is about engaging in pursuits apart from work that are stimulating and encourage cognitive development. As the children grew up, Lakshmi could no longer play with Jayashree and Krishna because she could no longer understand their games.

The world of make-believe and pretend play is alien to most children with autism. Such children find it easier to comprehend concrete concepts such as 'throw the ball into the bucket' rather than 'this bucket of water is a boat, I am the captain, and you are my soldier'.

While Jayashree and Krishna played captain and soldier, Lakshmi would watch in growing frustration due to two things. One, the game was not concrete, and two, her comprehension of language was way below theirs. At these times, Jayanthi was the mystery child who was never interested in what the others were doing and at peace within herself.

In the life of a person with autism, to play without being dependent on an individual for support assumes a lot of significance. While I noticed many uncommon things, such as Lakshmi's total lack of communication, Jayanthi gazing at the same object for hours on end, holding it close to her eyes, Jayashree and Krishna, when they were babies and up to the age of five, did not question anything. They would yank Lakshmi and Jayanthi around while playing and, like all children, become preoccupied with the child who responded. This meant Jayashree and Krishna would become preoccupied with playing with each other, Lakshmi would watch, and Jayanthi would have crawled away.

I refer to 'teddy chats' in a Margazhi story later in this book. These chats began when the children were around five or six years old. Discussions about the differences between them would come up, which I found painful. I did not have the wisdom that I have today. I did not have the acceptance of autism that I have today. With a painfully thudding heart, I would continue chatting with my children.

As the children grew older, the four of them became very close. They automatically gravitated towards each other. The secret purdah that had lain over the diagnosis of autism peeled off slowly but surely, and it exposed the rawness of embarrassment, pain, shame, hurt and helplessness in Jayashree and Krishna.

They would go down to play in the building compound and take Lakshmi and Jayanthi along. One day, Jayashree came back weeping, her face red with shock and humiliation.

'Amma, Lakshmi lifted her skirt and scratched herself inside her underwear. Amma, everyone was laughing at her. I brought her home. Amma, why did she do that?'

Sometimes there was militancy. 'I heard one uncle in the building calling Lakshmi mad because she was laughing to herself. Why not do a campaign door-to-door in the building and tell people that Lakshmi and Jayanthi are different, not mad.'

Somewhere at the back of my mind, a dormant octopus with frozen tentacles was awakening, bathed in the sunshine of the understanding of autism. I started chatting with CP—long discussions about what I wanted to do. Both of us had realised that the golden age of childhood—the make-believe world of seeing our four children wearing the same school uniforms, carrying school bags and lunch boxes, leaving home and returning at the same time—was over.

What would be the learning areas for Lakshmi and Jayanthi from the ages of nine to nineteen? Where did we think they should be by the age of twenty-one? What kind of adult life were we expecting them to lead when they were thirty plus? By that time, Jayashree and Krishna would be leading their own lives. CP and I would be far, far older.

Working backwards from this theory, I knew it was essential to have a training centre where teenagers with autism can move out of a school atmosphere into a college; where they are taught to handle freedom responsibly, where they work with co-workers instead of teachers, and learn skills that will equip them to live happily after the lifetime of their parents.

Did such a centre exist? No.

Ideas and thoughts swirled in my mind. I knew that Lakshmi and Jayanthi were not just two girls but part of a huge number of people with autism for whom building language and communication, vocational skills and independence in daily living were critical for their future happiness and security.

So, one day in 2013, I walked out of regular school, holding Lakshmi and Jayanthi's hands, and decided to do something. I started planning a full-length training programme.

It took me a year and a half to put my ideas together fully, from 2013 to the end of 2014. During this time, I developed a training programme for Lakshmi and Jayanthi at home, comprising self-help skills, language and communication, and pre-vocational skills. I was lucky to get the help of a lovely human being and special educator—Rinku Bhatia.

Rinku brought my programmes to life and one day, when we sat down to discuss work skills, we explored baking. Particularly because Lakshmi is so gifted in the kitchen. Rinku taught us to make simple chocolate cookies.

As the cookie project grew fast and beyond our expectations, I decided that this would be the fledgling business that the Together Foundation would run. Simple, quality products manufactured by people with disabilities, which will provide a bridge with the outside world and a mutually rewarding relationship.

The programme I devised was based on the concept of growing up, learning, and living a full life without academics, on the premise that without academics, there is still a lot one can do. My vision was to create a respectful environment where children with autism could grow up and learn to transition to living independently.

By this I didn't mean financial independence. Many individuals with autism will always remain financially dependent on their family or have other means of support. But there is much more to life than money. Money or not, we don't remain children all our lives. We grow up. We learn. We work. We laugh, cry, build relationships and need love and caring.

On this basis, a programme of work and life skills was planned for children with autism to find a way forward.

As I put it together, I documented the programme I created. I had detailed discussions with CP. He warned me that finding space for a centre would not be easy. He offered me space in our locality—three tiny shops that looked highly unappealing to me. I refused his offer.

'I want more space,' I said. 'I want trees and some open space where the team members can sit when they want a break.'

I wanted a grant. I wanted to support families of people with autism, irrespective of whether they could pay the fee or not. So there was no question of paying rent.

From my experience of securing space in Bangalore to run a free twenty-four-hour street animal helpline, I knew that it was possible. However, Mumbai proved to be tough. All people were ready to give me was one small room that could house two or three adults at best.

I went to the local government body and asked for space in an unoccupied building. The person in charge looked up at me.

'Madam, *uske taraf ankh uthake math dekhna* (Madam, don't look for such a thing).' After four or five months, I was dejected.

'Take this space, Sangeetha,' CP urged. 'Start, and someday, you will get your gardens and trees. I promise that I will convert the three shops into a bright and colourful space, with lot of ventilation.'

I also had to decide what kind of organisation the foundation would be. Again, I looked up links on the internet and found the name of a legal firm: Krishna and Saurastri. I called them up. They invited me for a meeting and helped me give form to my thoughts and vision without charging a fee. They continue to advise us even now. In 2015, we registered the organisation as a public charitable trust.

I requested CP to be the settlor for the organisation since he is a parent of children with special needs, had given the space at no cost and would continue to guide the organisation in financial integrity and policies. I wrote to Dr Amdekar. Never did I imagine that he would give us the time, knowledge and help that he did, despite his commitments. But he put his faith lock, stock and barrel in us and joined us as a trustee. He also invited his student, the social philanthropist Dr Anjali Tendulkar, to join the board of trustees.

CP and I waited quietly in Dr Amdekar's clinic when the soft-spoken and dignified Dr Tendulkar walked in. She listened quietly to our ideas and vision and turned to Dr Amdekar. 'I will be happy to join you and help the work that is going to be done,' she said.

That was it. The meeting was over in minutes. I can never forget her faith and willingness to support a cause.

While putting together my plans for Together Foundation, I visited centres of special needs learning all over Mumbai. I began from a small and lovely centre called Manuprem in Grant Road and made my way up to Andheri East. I met special educators, developmental paediatricians, occupational therapists and speech therapists. It was Sonali Gomes, a special educator, who told me, 'Sangeetha, your programme is ready. Why are you waiting? Start.'

But starting took some time. The premises needed to become operationally ready. CP broke down the small set of shops he had provided for the centre, promising to make the space vibrant, colourful and well-ventilated. He had listened to my dream of a garden with trees and benches where my students would take a break in the open air, rather than gaze at mobile phones. He also put in a strict system of financial control, making us accountable for every rupee we spent. This system has helped us keep unnecessary expenses to the minimum and ensure transparency.

Meanwhile, we got some help through a senior well-wisher, Mr Jagdeeshan, who introduced us to Puratos Food Ingredients India. The company operates a professional bakery to sample and prepare mixes for the bakery and patisserie sectors, etc., of the food industry. They allowed us to bake on Saturdays and spent a lot of time guiding us. The experience was invaluable. Lakshmi and Jayanthi were the first to join the programme officially under the Together brand. Sonali Gomes brought in some of her students as well. Eventually, the premises of the centre were ready and we moved in.

In the beginning, the centre had hardly any takers since our programme was not based on academics. Lakshmi and Jayanthi were the first students, and Jayashree and Krishna our first volunteers. Later that year, three more students joined.

As we expanded and parents came to know about our work, the number of admissions increased. So did the number of teachers.

We began with a microwave oven and a small bakery. I made a memorable visit to the corporate office of Godrej Nature's Basket in Vikhroli, Mumbai. They were kind and courteous but refused to stock our products. 'Madam, where is the FSSAI registration?'

With their words ringing in my ears and clutching the beautifully designed cookie boxes that Kiran Khalap's chlorophyll brand consultancy had made for us, I returned to our centre. One and a half years later, we had commercial baking equipment, an FSSAI registration, two consultant chefs—Mrudula Putcha and

Rinal Karvat—and ten products in the bakery. From one to ten to thirty-five products in ten years, Together grew slowly and steadily.

Among our differently abled team members, there were a few who were not suited to work in a bakery. I started borrowing ideas from everywhere. I learnt, for example, that Autism Ashram has a paper plate manufacturing machine. We bought one. Someone asked us if we made paper bags. We brought out a line of beautiful block-printed gift bags. Two years later, we began cloth bags. After the outbreak of the COVID-19 pandemic, when there was no work in sight, the teachers and I contacted medical shops who agreed to buy brown paper bags from us. We began work all over again.

The most enthralling, uplifting and motivational experience I had was when I began scouting for work that our team members could do. On my way back from yet another unsuccessful attempt to get work, I spotted the bright red board of Creative Handicrafts, a clothing company that empowers women from the rural belt. I walked in, introduced myself, and explained that I was looking for work for our team members.

'Mr Joseph, our director, will meet you.'

I walked into his cabin. He listened to me and said, 'Will you be okay with threading labels for us?'

'Yes, sir. I would like to see the process.'

He showed me. I agreed.

He sent me back with a carton of one thousand labels.

For ten years, we have continued to thread labels for Creative Handicrafts.

We opened a registered shop on our premises and sold our bakery products, our bags, plates, festive handicrafts, fresh foods like idlis and toasted sandwiches. We also began doing data entry for a bank.

In 2016, our fee was Rs 15,000 a month. We had arrived at this figure based on the costs we incurred for teachers' salaries, teaching aids, electricity, maintenance, etc. Dr Anjali Tendulkar became our patron saint, paving the way for us to offer our services to low-income families at a nominal fee from day one. Her grant to Together ensured that we could take in families that could not pay more than Rs 500 a month. It took us three years to start receiving funds from institutions, corporates and individuals. Today, grants from Tata Investment Corporation Ltd, Perowshaw Dhunjishaw Bolton Charities, and several individual well-wishers allow us to offer a lower fee of Rs 4,000 for all families and a subsidised fee for needy families.

During this time, I forgot about everything else to the exclusion of Together. We had few students and therefore minimal staff. So I was designing content, teaching, planning and handling administrative duties. I worked at a feverish pace with a team of teachers to keep up with the varying requirements of the families that approached us for training programmes.

Simultaneously, I enrolled for training programmes and courses in both autism and other special needs and counselling. I am now a cognitive behaviour therapist for adults with autism, certified Young Adults Provider at UCLA Peers, which provides evidence-based social skills training for youth with neural developmental disabilities, and have completed the Don Bosco Post Graduate Diploma in Integrated Education and Counselling. I hold a South Asian Diploma in Narrative Practices, which is offered by Narrative Practices India, a collective that explores narrative ideas in diverse contexts.

As the organisation grew, I found myself in need of a mentor. Sheela Sinha agreed to join our board of trustees. She had retired as Director of Education at the Helen Keller Institute of the Deaf and Deafblind. She was kindness itself and over the next two years, she helped me set processes in place.

Later, we were bolstered by the addition of one more trustee, a person who had been a guiding force from the time we founded Together: Jaya Rangarajan. She had been the principal of Little Angels 'Saplings' School for children with special needs. I persuaded her to join us formally and help steer the path ahead.

On a chance visit to Delhi, I sought a meeting with Kavita Sharma, the founder of Prayas, a centre for computer learning for children and adults with autism. Over a delicious breakfast at her home, she told me, 'Sangeetha, it's great you want to train your students in computer skills. You can access all our programmes on our website free of cost.'

I looked at her and marvelled at the service she had offered the community. This was in the year 2014. Six years later, I got the opportunity to follow in Kavita's footsteps. At the peak of the lockdown, we collated all the teaching programmes we had conducted since Together Foundation's inception, and uploaded them on our website, enabling free access for parents and professionals.

Today, Together Foundation's board of trustees comprises Professor Emeritus Dr Y.K. Amdekar, Dr Anjali Tendulkar, Ms Sheela Sinha, Ms Jaya Rangarajan, Dr Pramod Krishnan (adult neurologist), Dr Leena Deshpande (developmental paediatrician) and Mr Vijay Krishnamurthy (parent member of The Together Community).

My children had not expected their mother to embrace the vision of Together Foundation so fiercely. I developed teaching programmes that help individuals with autism to learn work and life skills. I began by teaching our team of adults, went on to train the teachers, and continued to implement the programmes on a larger scale. Apart from regular work skill programmes, I took a great deal of time to design three programmes for Together: Talktime, Phone a Friend with Autism and AutiTales. Talktime is an audio-visual programme that empowers communication on a range of everyday topics. Phone a Friend with Autism is an ambitious programme that had the teachers looking at me with raised eyebrows. Nevertheless, we initiated contact with the close friends and family members of our adults and carried out a training programme in video calling that has built phone buddies across the country for individuals with autism. After seven years of multiple efforts to engage in storytelling, I took the help of Kiran

Khalap's team at chlorophyll brand consultancy and conceptualised AutiTales, interactive stories for people with autism that can be accessed through a free-to-download Android app.

CP is an incredibly tough mentor. As the person who leads the organisation, my mind and heart dart in a thousand directions, wanting to do so many things at once. CP's implacable logic and multiple reminders that we are handling 'public money' that must be utilised for maximum and collective good have helped the organisation to sustain and expand its initiatives.

Today, while I continue to be involved with the centre, I do not visit it every day. I manage it remotely, and the system augurs well for the future. I am available on call for teachers and parents anytime. Our teaching programmes are planned in advance, documented, available for free access and shared with parents. We encourage and promote transparency in work practices. Our centre is monitored by CCTV cameras, and parents have access to CCTV footage. Parents are allowed to enter the centre without prior appointments and see their child at work (provided they do not cause any disruption). Meetings and discussions with teachers are held both online and offline only by prior appointment (unless it is anything urgent concerning the adult's wellbeing).

I enjoy developing teaching programmes and sharing with teachers through demos and workshops. I continue to conceptualise programmes for the centre, but I don't do it alone anymore. The teachers play a significant role.

My focus is now on transition planning for adults with autism to prepare for independent living. I work with a team of counsellors and special educators to help parents move towards this goal. I am completely immersed in helping to establish our residential project, The Together Community at Hosur, which Lakshmi and Jayanthi will also join. Forty families and adults with special needs will be moving in, to start a life of supported and independent living. It is a huge milestone in our lives and something for which I thank CP and Vedaanta Senior Living with hands folded in gratitude. No matter how hard I have worked or am willing to in the future, I depend on CP to help fulfil my dreams in a sustainable and practical manner.

The year 2025 had not even turned a month old when I saw a news article about a family of four, including two children, who had died by suicide, one of the causes of which was the stress of having a child with autism. That night, as I sat to write my Margazhi story for the next morning, I could not find humour or joy or calm in my pen. This family needed to be addressed and I began writing. As I wrote, chronicling our own family story when autism walked in through our door, the answer also came.

9
Dreams come true ... at a price

CREATING AN INDEPENDENT HOME FOR LAKSHMI AND JAYANTHI, and planning for their security in their adult years became increasingly important to me. I had to approach CP several times over a few years to explore this idea. As a father, he could not envisage his home without the children, more so Lakshmi and Jayanthi as autism makes it daunting to imagine an independent life for them.

Eventually, when our daughters were about eight and a half years old, I persuaded CP to think about it, and we made our first visit to a residential community. He was disturbed at the thought of coming face to face with adults with autism living away from their parents. It took me time to convince him that we would not be giving our children away but helping them to live happily without us.

The residential home we visited was Friends of Camphill in Bangalore. When I called them, Francis Aradhya came to the phone.

At first, she misunderstood my intention. 'We don't take such young children, Sangeetha,' she said.

'Francis, I am not looking for admission but want to know about starting a group home.'

'Come over.'

When CP and I left for Friends of Camphill, we were quiet, a maelstrom of emotions surging within us. It would be our first time meeting adults with disabilities—people with special needs who were not living with their parents. We didn't know what to call the place. Was it a facility? A caregivers' environment? A hostel? An institution? A dormitory? Words like these were fighting for space in our minds.

But when we got there, what followed was four hours of the most natural, interactive and purposeful meetings that CP and I have ever had.

We met Francis, her husband Anantha Aradhya, and the residents of Camphill. Over a cup of tea, Francis gently involved every resident in conversation, providing us with a masterclass on the leisurely and unhurried communication that is so vital for people with special needs.

The seeds of Together Foundation were sown that day. I knew we could not start a group home overnight, but I knew where and what to begin with.

At Friends of Camphill, we saw the residence, we saw the workspaces, the organic garden and the kitchen, where the cook was being assisted by a couple of the residents who were rolling out chapatis.

When we moved out of the kitchen to a long porch with a bench, I noticed the same young lady who had been assisting the cook in the kitchen now sitting there. Just sitting quietly, at rest.

'Francis, is she not the same person who was inside the kitchen?'
'Yes.'
'How come she is here?'
Francis laughed.
'Oh, she sits here every day. She loves to have an extra chapati as a treat. Sometimes she gets one. Sometimes she doesn't.'

I paused right there, unable to move forward. There was so much love, humour and ease in Francis's voice. I can hear it even now.

My voice, my heart, everything clenched painfully in that one second. I could imagine my Lakshmi, my Tomato who loves her food, sitting on that bench, waiting for a chapati that she sometimes would get and sometimes would not.

If this was not a home, then what is? A group home is a home that raises, nurtures, embraces, scolds, loves, corrects, hugs and helps us grow and live our lives till our last day.

When we look at a group home, we tend to evaluate the rooms, the space, the bedding, the bathrooms, the food. We ask, is there a cook, is there housekeeping, is there security, are there vocational activities, is there enough staff? We keep looking for a place where our biggest question is: will my child get everything she wants here?

What we cannot see with the physical eye but can only experience and must also look for is this: Is there care? Is there love? Is there laughter? Is there understanding? Do people here know each other? Looking at each other's faces, can they sense, 'She is not okay, let me spend some more time with her?' Can they sense and feel peace and happiness in each other? Does that peace and happiness lie in an extra chapati?

No.

In my home, I have lost count of the number of times Lakshmi goes foraging in the kitchen for something extra to eat. Sometimes she finds something. Sometimes she does not. But Lakshmi is at home with us. I become militant when I think about Lakshmi in a group home. If she wants an extra chapati, she must have it.

But that's room service, not a home.

I made my way out of Camphill with composure and so did CP. We stood outside, near our car, unable to say anything to each other. Maybe thirty minutes passed. Then we got into the car and drove away.

It has been ten years since I visited Camphill but the lessons of love, respect, protection, sharing and calmness that CP and I learnt there are fresh in our minds and hearts, giving us the strength, resolve and energy to keep striving on our path.

After we visited Friends of Camphill, CP agreed to at least contemplate setting up a model for a group home. However, being a banker, he had innumerable questions about how to ensure the long-term sustainability of the project. While he admired my passion and dedication, he was clear that The Together Community would be a collaboratively run model and not my responsibility alone.

We spent many years discussing the most efficient way to run a community for adults with autism on a long-term and sustainable basis.

Over a period of eight years, we visited and spent hours at various residential projects across India. There was a lot to learn, and we had several ideas that we wanted to implement. Both of us were keen to establish a project that would be connected with the rest of society and yet give our friends with autism their independence and privacy. A place where parents could live in the same campus and yet give space to their children with autism to live independently. We also wanted to tie up with a developer and service provider to ensure quality and sustenance of services.

I was ready to take an apartment in Mumbai and start a small residential project. CP refused. He was adamant about having a model that would assuredly stand the test of time for eighty to a hundred years. He wanted me to get parents on board who would invest in a shared dream.

That was a no go. Where would I find these mythical parents?

We argued back and forth on the subject of the community and had key interactions with Aparna Das at Arunima, Merry Barua at Ananda, and A.K. Kundra at Autism Ashram, all of whom generously shared nuggets of wisdom with us. Like a gunshot, Mr Kundra asked us, 'Do you have faith in what you want to do? Why would you want others to invest in your dream? Do not wait for others. Start. Others will join you.'

Late one evening, when we were returning from the airport, we hit upon the thought that the management of the community should not be done by Together Foundation. The core area of the foundation's expertise lies with specific services for people with disabilities. Instead, we zeroed in on a model based on senior living communities because many of the services offered by them are useful for people with special needs. Once those factors were taken care of, we thought, the community would be managed efficiently and for the long run.

We had spent valuable time trying to establish the project in Mumbai. A further couple of years passed before I felt we should explore Bangalore. That made it five years since we first had the idea. I had to knock at CP's door for a very long time before he agreed to even think of relocating from Mumbai. His logic and my passion were at loggerheads, in trying to establish the community.

'Who will develop it?' CP challenged me.

Not for one minute, ever, had he reassured me, 'Don't worry, it will work out.' Instead, he found the loopholes in every alternative I presented to him.

One Sunday, I persuaded CP to join me in speaking to a long list of senior living services in Bangalore—at least thirty organisations. CP watched as, one by one, everyone refused me politely.

'Sorry, we cannot accommodate special needs in our project.'

The next day, I got a response from Vedaanta Senior Living. I called CP excitedly.

'Forget it, they must not have understood your requirements.'

'CP, they called again.'

'Their projects are full. They can't accommodate us.'

'CP, their CEO called me and will meet us online.'

'Okay.'

It has not been easy for me to win CP's cooperation and support while trying to sow the seeds of our project. However, once CP met Vedaanta and was convinced that they were serious about helping us establish, develop and manage the project, there was no looking back. I took a backseat as CP delved into the commercial and technical aspects of the project, pored over every minute aspect, and created the blueprint of our residential project that Kiran Khalap named for us: The Together Community.

What are CP's strengths? He has more than thirty years of banking experience and a strong emphasis on accountability. A gritty childhood taught him to empathise with those who are needy, that nothing comes free, and that everything must be evaluated emotionlessly and practically. He has an eye for detail and an ability to make me feel like an earthworm, effortlessly.

My strengths are my understanding of autism that no textbook will teach you, my capacity to work relentlessly, my passion for achieving something that I believe in by never giving up, my belief in transparent work systems, my joy in sharing with families and friends with autism, my skills in designing and implementing creative autism teaching programmes, and my faith in CP despite his difficult personality.

Together, we are a force to be reckoned with.

We decided to do the project with Vedaanta. Over the next eighteen months, we had several meetings with them. We also consulted legal experts and finalised the plans.

The idea behind The Together Community was that parents would buy and own a villa in the community and pay a deposit for a studio apartment for their adult child with special needs. This studio apartment would be in a building with other such apartments, where all the adult children with special needs would live independently, away from their families but with their families close by. The deposit for the apartment, we decided, would reside with The Together Parents' Welfare Trust since all the special adults would come under the collective care of all the parents.

The staff of the community would be recruited by Vedaanta Senior Living. But in areas pertaining to direct support professionals, such as caregivers for the adult children with special needs, Vedaanta would do the recruitment with support from Together Foundation. In addition, Together Foundation would ensure caregiver training in special needs and sensitisation of all staff members in the wider community.

Even the costs were worked out in all seriousness and not from the point of view of marketability. That's because the parents had to know what resources they would require, both as a one-time payment for the villa and apartment and as the monthly payments they would have to make thereafter. They needed this information to help them plan the means to meet their expenses.

To reach out to the parents, we created a one-of-its-kind project brochure with complete details of the project, its management and its financials. The brochure included FAQs and we circulated it among communities of parents of children with special needs. We held webinars and Zoom meetings with parents and organised in-person interactions in Mumbai and Bangalore.

Parents who were interested were asked to fill in an online application form. Then our team, which consisted of CP, me and the Vedaanta directors, met every interested parent one on one in an online meeting. This gave the parents privacy to discuss their requirements and ask questions. Vedaanta has a team that organises site visits, which led the parents around the site. The last step was an online meeting with our medical committee that consisted of an adult psychiatrist, an adult neurologist, a paediatrician, and our biggest guru, Dr Y.K. Amdekar. After this interaction with the medical committee, the parents felt assured that The Together Community could do justice to the requirements of their adult children with special needs.

The Together Community at Hosur provides an environment where parents and their children with special needs can live in a shared campus and yet walk the path of independent living. It is equipped with manifold facilities for a well-rounded life: a comfortable home, ample support, a team that empowers, proximity to family, consistent work opportunities, nutritious food, healthcare, physical engagement, community engagement, shopping, meals out and leisure options. However, the fabric binding these services in order to create a home will be made of something intangible.

The Together Community will not be merely a space for adult children with autism to live in after their parents are gone. It will be a home.

What is a home? A home is a place where a person stays in his or her room, has a TV in the room, watches TV, lies down, sleeps, has a cupboard, has a bathroom and all of that. These elements don't make it a home. Home is a place where a person gets up in the morning and hears voices. Home is where, when a person steps out of their room, they see people moving around. There is somebody who calls out to them. There is somebody who waves at them and they wave back at. There is someone they can ask for help. There is someone who says, 'Happy Diwali!' There is somebody who says, 'Do you know we are going for a picnic today?'

Home is where you are guided gently, where you are loved and cared for, where somebody knows or at least wants to know, 'Did you sleep well at night? Are you alright? Why are you looking a little pale today?'

Home is where you know each other. You care for each other and you know how the other person is doing.

This is The Together Community. This is our dream, our vision. This is how we will run the place.

Then, one night, CP called me.

He was in Bangalore. He asked me to fly there the next morning. We met on the way to the site of the project. There, CP and our Vedaanta colleagues informed me that the site was at risk.

I argued with the Vedaanta executives relentlessly. It was a no go. Illegal quarrying work had begun that could go on for years, putting the health of all the residents of The Together Community at risk. With CP and Vedaanta, I toured the site, spoke to locals, met environmental and legal experts. In frustration, I rounded on CP. 'How could you let this happen? There are other parents who have put their hope and faith in us.' I was furious and held him fully responsible for the mess we were in.

I could not bear to be in the same space as him, yet I knew that if this project could be restored, it would happen through him. I had known this several years earlier, when I decided that we would establish a residential community. Why? Because it's not enough to care. It's not enough to teach or conceptualise or design or provide the most ethically delivered services for autism. You also need a logical, dispassionate mind that cares but also applies math and logic to the care. It's very important to have someone who will always make you feel uncomfortable, who will never let you become complacent. Someone who will both find and help fix loopholes.

It was 26 March 2023, and it was the single most debilitating moment of my life since the children were born.

It took CP a long time to convince me that all was not lost and that we could begin again. I refused to return to Mumbai and pledged to stay put in Bangalore till the project was secure. CP went back to Mumbai to fetch Lakshmi and Jayanthi to Bangalore. After installing us in a service apartment, CP returned to Mumbai and continued working on securing an alternate site.

I have always emphasised transparency in work and spoke to our parent members without any delay. I told them about the crisis we were facing and asked CP to reassure them about the way ahead.

And yes, we made a transition successfully. CP and Vedaanta together helped me tour and finalise a new site for our project at Hosur, in a thirty-five-acre gated community. On the border of Tamil Nadu and Karnataka, Hosur is popularly known as Greater Bengaluru due to its proximity to the city of Bengaluru. What drew me to this site at Sri Shankara Colony at Hosur was that Vedaanta is already established securely there, with a senior living project in the same campus. Filled with greenery and dotted with tiny temples, the campus is serene and calming. I took a cab from The Together Community site at Sri Shankara Colony and plotted the travelling time to various places of importance for our special adults.

Nearest hospital: Ten minutes.

Nearest multi-specialty hospital: Twenty-five minutes.

Narayana Hruduyalaya: Forty-five minutes.

Nearest bakery to go to for a quick bite, entrancingly named Little England: Fifteen minutes.

Nearest restaurant for a full meal: Forty minutes.
Shopping for clothes and odds and ends: Forty minutes.
Are there local picnic spots? Yes.
Is there regular connectivity to people apart from parents and caregivers? Yes.
Are there opportunities to engage with local businesses and industries? Yes.

My eyes welled with tears when I entered Sri Shankara Colony for the first time. The stress of losing our project had taken a toll on me. My composure was cracking at the edges. At the entrance to the colony, right opposite the proposed construction of The Together Community, I saw my old friend. I saw the one who had held my hands silently through my most painful years, the one who helped my family stick together through the most difficult times. Who, without saying a word to me, had helped me become a better version of myself. I saw a simple temple dedicated to Sri Sathya Sai Baba.

The Together Community will go live in April 2026. Forty families of forty individuals with autism and special needs will move into The Together Community. Together Foundation will provide disability-specific services. Vedaanta Senior Living will develop and manage the community across all areas. The parent group will mentor, supervise and nurture the community.

Over the years, CP and I have had to create a new normal in our fragile relationship. It's been a long time since I promoted him to a friend since our early years of strife and struggle. We settled into the comfortable roles of 'you hardworking Daddy and me hardworking Mummy'. Then we began to smile at each other as our children grew and helped us slowly merge the lines of anxiety with little joys and normal experiences like eating out and holidays. Then came our combined role at Together Foundation where CP provided the space and financial controls while I developed and established an organisation.

Now, at this moment in time, all the lines have merged. This project is going to mean living together for the rest of our lives, working together and taking ownership of a community. From day one, we planned a joint governance of the project along with every parent who joins the community, thus paving the way for the continuity of the project much beyond the Chakrapani family.

However, both CP and I know that we must put our combined might into creating an environment, a culture and a narrative that will uphold, protect and nurture the lives of every special adult at The Together Community. The two of us, along with our children, are bound by one more invisible thread of commitment towards each other and the community.

10
Scraping through as a family

AS THE CHILDREN FINALLY STAND BEFORE US AS ADULTS, CP AND I have learnt that we have to let them go.

Jayashree and Krishna are at a turning point in their lives as they turn twenty-one. They will soon complete their graduation and choose the paths they want to take. They may opt for higher studies or take up work, and only time will tell us where they will be located. We have tried our best to invest them with values of empathy, self-reliance, the ability to ask for help and the courage to walk alone. We have expressed our solidarity and support, no matter where they are.

Lakshmi has prospered in the bakery at Together Foundation. She has cooked and rolled and kneaded and baked and found her calling. She lends herself to all areas of the foundation and is intensely devoted to her teachers and co-workers. For her, work is worship, the centre her temple, and the teachers her gods.

Jayanthi has worked in groups to prepare handicraft products. She has also done basic preparation work at the bakery. However, she has found her niche in manufacturing paper bags for medical stores and in data entry. Jayanthi, like many others, does not recognise all the alphabets. However, she types by matching shapes and patterns. She maintains her space wherever she goes.

She blends, she follows, she cooperates, and yet there is a saintly aloofness about her that hints at an other-worldliness.

I will move to Hosur and begin work from scratch all over again. CP will move back and forth since he has compelling ties in Mumbai. This home will never be the same again. We will never get these days again. We will have to find happiness and comfort and togetherness in the individual paths that lie ahead of us and continue to support each other, wherever we may be.

How do we take a joint decision with our child when the two of us are not equals? When we are stronger than them? When we are more competent and intellectually on a better footing?

We start by increasing their readiness to explore the world, one step at a time, by being there for them and yet giving them the space to make a happy world for themselves.

With us. And without us.

Our four children have shown us in their own ways that they are ready for autonomy over their lives. Krishna quite simply does what he wants to do and does not do what he does not want to do, irrespective of how sane he might appear to us or not. Jayashree pretends to ask and then does what she wants to do, though she resembles Jayanthi in her perceptible gentleness.

Lakshmi has launched into outright rebellion, leaving the house to go shopping without informing us. She also tries to make decisions for us in extremely personal choices, such as what we should wear. Jayanthi engages in more juvenile pursuits, like flinging things outside the windows, and drinking tea and coffee that belongs to others. As Anil bhaiya says, '*Teeno bade ho gaye. Ek Jayanthi hai jo bachchi hai* (Three of them have grown up. Only Jayanthi remains a child).'

Years ago, Shah Rukh Khan songs would play on a loop for hours on end at our home. Krishna would wrestle with Lakshmi and change the channel. Jayashree would try to persuade Lakshmi to watch *Dance Pe Chance Mar Le* on her iPad. Jayanthi would watch the battle for the remote control peaceably. Her only contribution so far has been to throw the remote from the seventh floor.

Nowadays, Krishna does not wrestle with Lakshmi for the remote. Lakshmi rarely watches *Dance Pe Chance* .... She logs into YouTube when she wants.

Each one of these four has begun making her or his own path. Every time they meet, they will discover new things about each other.

What will bind them forever?

Sharing the womb, knowing what makes the other person tick and accepting that they will all grow up and mature.

With autism and without.

What binds them together can never be captured in words. A Shah Rukh Khan song is enough.

11
Jai Rajinikanth!

DO YOU KNOW HOW I GO TO SLEEP EVERY NIGHT? WITH Rajinikanth on my phone.

Inevitably, thoughts about my four children and anxiety about their future crowd my mind. Many a time, tears burn their passage down my throat as I try to compose myself. So I have a fund of Rajinikanth jokes and videos of impossible stunts performed by him on my phone. I watch a couple of them, say 'Jai Rajinikanth', tightly close my eyes and go to sleep.

It is definite that the multitude of challenges that presented themselves before us affected both CP and me. If not, would we have behaved like Romeo and Juliet? I don't know. I know that we are comrades at heart, brought together to raise this family of four young, wonderful people.

Two people who need to guide and nurture these children through their delicate plunge into adulthood. Two people who instinctively think alike and have the gumption to handle challenges head on. What does the future hold for us? I don't know, just as I am unaware of the challenges that await us.

I am not being negative. It's just that in the life story of two youngsters with autism and two neurotypical youngsters of the same age, the next decade is going to be vital in helping them find their bearings and learning to let go while they carve their individual destinies.

Will CP and I always hold our battle-scarred hands together? Will the children always remain united? I like to believe so, even though adulthood will impose its own set of requirements, particularly on Jayashree and Krishna. These golden days of sitting happily in one room, each doing his or her own thing will not last for long. All four of them will go their own ways.

But the homespun values we have lived by, the stories of our childhood, the failures and successes that both CP and I have shared with our children, their own journey of grit and determination from the womb and beyond, will keep the pact of love, trust and support strong and patent between them. We may not be perfectly sewn together. Maybe a tear here, maybe a jagged edge there, but we are strong enough to continue weathering storms and holding an umbrella of hope above our collective heads.

Epilogue

EVERY MORNING, AFTER COOKING AND MAKING LUNCH BOXES FOR CP and my daughters, I savour a cup of coffee. This is normally the safest time for the kids to tell me dangerous things like, 'I don't want the baingan you've made today', and CP to fan the flames with, 'Oh, you've made mor kozhambu today, no rasam?'

Only because of the coffee that has hit my alimentary canal, I smile cooperatively, instead of asking my family members to start walking towards Africa or wherever in search of chutney or whatever they want to eat.

Yesterday, Jayashree and I chatted over my coffee about my favourite animal, the elephant.

With a wealth of feeling, I told her, 'Jayashree, elephants experience and express an enormous depth of emotions. They run towards each other in joy at a reunion. The most important event is the arrival of a newborn. They form a ring around the mother and her baby, they help her bring her baby up and form a group of lifelong babysitters. These mothers who babysit in need are called "allomothers". This way, every baby elephant is nurtured by several parents and not one.'

'Like your group home na, Amma?' Jayashree asked in her bell-like voice that clanged with resounding clarity in that moment.

I gazed at her in silence as images of a group of parents of children with autism flashed before my eyes. Some old and some young, with hearts full of love and hope and compassion and determination. A group of adults: some quiet, some talkative, some doe-like, some boisterous. With eyes full of trust, hearts full of innocence, and with hardworking hands and legs and minds.

Every child is my child. My child is everyone's child.

Loka samastha sukhino bhavanthu.

The elephants discovered it long before us.

We just need to follow.

MARGAZHI STORIES

Guess what we got ourselves as a gift for this Diwali? A mesh for the windows!

Around two weeks ago, I sat down to wrap up the accounts for Together Foundation. CP's dictum is, 'When you choose to run a non-profit organisation, your accounts must be verifiable on an everyday basis. Remember that the words "approximate" and "etc." don't exist.'

I must have been engrossed in the task because Jayanthi decided to drop my mobile phone out of the window. We are on the seventh floor. I had no idea what had happened and where my phone was, and searched frantically till the doorbell rang. The lady who clears the building garbage stood there with a singularly sympathetic smile as she held out the remains of my phone. She said, '*Sim card theek hi hoga* (The sim card should be okay).'

CP was unsympathetic and demoted me from my Samsung Note 1/2/whatever to a Mohenjo-daro–Harappa variety of phone. He also advised me to start developing telepathic communication since this would be the last phone he would replace.

My dad has started placing his phone on the highest bookshelf. He says, 'I got my first mobile when I was sixty-two years old. I can't afford to buy phones like bread and biscuits.'

The helpers held a joint conference and created a locker in the kitchen where they store their mobiles.

CP called a mesh supplier and much to the supplier's amazement, first tried to insert a phone, pencil and eraser through the mesh before he said, 'Okay, *laga do* (Fix it).'

I started wearing big bindis in my first year of college, 1991, in Delhi. My mother gawked at me.

'Sangeetha, what is this?'

'Bindi.'

'*Enakku theriyum* (I know). It makes you look older. Plus, why a salwar–kameez all the time? What about the jeans Appa bought for you when he went to the US and all of us garlanded him at the airport and told everyone we knew, including the watchman, that Appa went to the US?'

'Amma, I climbed into the jeans. It was horrible. Give me my salwar–kameez and dupatta any day.'

Much later, after marriage and quads, I called Amma from Mahabaleshwar where I was on holiday. 'Do you know someone thought I am a TV serial actor?'

She was not impressed but grudgingly said, 'It's because of your TV serial bindis. But they look nice on you, Sangeetha.'

My mother always bemoaned the fact that I never wore bangles. 'Sangeetha, you are serving food to CP without bangles. I am not happy.'

'Shall I ask him to serve himself? Amma, I find bangles irritating.'

The day I lost her, she and I had travelled by ambulance from home to hospital. She was peaceful because she had seen my father and held his hand: the man who was the fulcrum of her existence. When we reached the hospital, her hands were in mine and grew cold in my grasp. I was talking to her, singing Sai bhajans for her. At one point, I took the bangles from her wrists and slipped them onto my bare wrists. Never have they left me since then.

More than ten years have passed. Amma's loss, the ambulance ride and her bangles are etched in my memory. My bindis and the jeans my daughters wear make me think of my mother with a smile.

Today, I have a strange mix of jewellery. My gold earrings are safeguarded zealously, because Lakshmi gives away any gold that she finds. Her strategy is more noble than Ashoka's after the

Kalinga war. She just takes the gold jewellery and offers it to the random people she meets in the lift or while on a walk.

I started looking for faux jewellery and by some chance, saw a bunch of cute earrings that looked like a lot of fun.

Terracotta jhumkas for Lakshmi.

Mosambi-, watermelon- and strawberry-shaped earrings for Jayanthi.

Owl-shaped earrings for Jayashree.

Tiny earrings in oxidised metal in the shape of a cycle!

I bought the cycle earrings for myself.

One hundred rupees and impossibly cute.

I wore the cycle earrings and went out a few days ago. I met CP outside the elevator. He had just got back from work. He blinked. 'What are you wearing in your ears?'

'Cycles!' I said happily.

'Cycles?'

'Are they not cute? Only a hundred rupees!'

'Then why go to Bhima, Kalyan and Joyalukkas if this is your end goal?'

'See, CP, they make me feel happy and light-hearted.'

I know CP well and quickly clambered into the car before he could say, 'Take Lakshmi or Jayanthi's cycle. It won't cost you even a hundred rupees and will make you feel light in more ways than one.'

As a mother, I have been saying 'Sorry' on behalf of Lakshmi and Jayanthi since 2006.

'Sorry, Lakshmi cut your dupatta with the craft scissors while you were writing on the blackboard.' (Give Lakshmi a craft box with old newspaper, scissors, scrapbook and glue.)

'Sorry, Jayanthi will need lots of help with her snack box.' (Start snack box practice at home for Jayanthi. Get her to open the box, eat the contents and put the lid back on.)

'Sorry, Lakshmi managed to grab the slice of cake from Ronit and ate it up.' (Make a birthday visual schedule for Lakshmi showing what to expect at a birthday party and what to do.)

'Sorry, Jayanthi forgot to wear her shoes to school today and is wearing floaters.' (Make a visual schedule for Jayanthi showing a bag, shoes, snack box and hanky. She has to check she has all of these things before she leaves home.)

'Sorry, Lakshmi grabbed fries from you in the lift while going down for a walk in our building.' (Discuss behaviour with Lakshmi, negotiate with a friend who will strategically appear in the lift every day for one week, eating fries or chips or chocolate, and help Lakshmi deal with it. Give Lakshmi a treat schedule at home to help her ask for treats.)

'Sorry, Jayanthi started howling in the middle of the family outing. Her thighs were itchy and she could not walk.' (Teach Jayanthi to point to her thighs when they itch. Keep coconut oil and Vaseline in the bathroom. Teach her to apply one or the other on her inner thighs.)

When they were children, I could use a very firm voice and tell them what would work and what would not.

Ever since they've turned thirteen, I've noticed subtle shifts in their personalities.

More assertiveness.

'I WILL bang the bathroom door shut,' Jayanthi says.

'I will NOT eat this sabzi,' says Lakshmi.

I respect this but I have trained myself to treat them as grown-ups and teach them to treat me as one.

I will not talk to them with a baby voice. ('Lakshmi is a good girl' and things like that.)

I will give them choices. ('Do you want this sabzi?')

I will not patronise them. (Rather than 'Come, I will take you for a walk', I say, 'Shall we go for a walk?')

I will not let them push me around. ('No, you can't enter my room when I have a meeting. No, you can't eat from my plate. This is my share.')

I will love them and cherish them while respecting their right to privacy. ('No, I will not enter the bathroom to help you bathe when you have no clothes on. Put on your two-piece swimsuit and I will come in.')

Yes, I love you and will hug you and cherish you.

But I will not kiss you and touch you all over your body or let you touch me anywhere, so you understand what age-appropriate touch means.

I am not only your mother. There will always be a 'but' between us that will help us grow up and coexist with others.

Among the kids, Krishna was the only one to be named before birth. We had decided on Krishna's name—even before we knew of the baby's gender—as part of negotiations with the divine to help the baby make it. The NICU nurses gave him a nickname—Elephant—and made colourful cards for his incubator, with sketches of elephants, flutes, etc. At home, when I get along with him, I call him 'Yanai papa', Tamil for baby elephant.

Lakshmi was nicknamed Tomato for her bright skin and sparkling eyes. Her first check-up after being discharged after birth was at Holy Spirit Hospital in Andheri East. CP and I walked in, holding one baby each, followed by two ayahs carrying the other two. My heart was thumping with anxiety and all my attention was on the thought, 'What are they going to say when they see Krishna? Will they be satisfied with his growth?'

CP was watching our little retinue of one baby with one adult and had no time to reflect. Tomato sat in my arms like a Kashmir apple and looked around with curious eyes. The doctor hefted her into his arms and announced, 'This baby needs to go on a diet.'

Lakshmi has a way of doing things. After a movie, when the lights go on, she briskly announces, 'Wakey, wakey, wakey! Good morning!' She loves Sai Baba. When we stopped at a beautiful riverside area in Himachal, she expressed her joy by bursting into song and singing Sai bhajans. She is our own homegrown Tomato!

Jayanthi was nicknamed Squirrel, for her habit of curling up into a small ball. Our own in-house Greta Garbo, Jayanthi is famous for disappearing suddenly and giving us lovely memories of organising frantic search parties for her. She commands personalised services for each of her earthly needs—someone needs to pass over her shoes, carry her plate because she won't handle hot food, and even remind her to eat. So CP and I cleverly trained the other three to periodically shout, 'Jayanthi, eat!' during meals. Her inner peace, blissful smile and innate composure even when we tick her off make us feel that it is we who need intervention. Half an hour spent with her makes us question all the needless things we worry about. She is our own Gautam Buddha in training mode.

Nicknamed Butterfly, Jayashree is our minstrel of mercy, helping all of us find our misplaced things as she briskly manages to lose hers. She has a unique perspective. When we made greeting cards for Sai Baba, she said, 'There is no need to post them. If you believe in him, the letters will leave your hands and fly to Puttaparthi by themselves.' All of us got worried at this tall order.

As we got our Ganapati ready for visarjan, she said that there was no need to say bye forever because she has taken his phone number. Her rendition of the English language set our teeth on edge: 'My teacher taughten me, she gaven me, tolden me.' Our English professor in the making, Jayashree is our imperfectly perfect child.

An idea can change your life.

I was at the grocery store with Jayanthi. She wanted Frooti and was trying to figure out a way to ask for it, knowing full well that I would not cooperate till she either signed or gestured. The shopkeeper, watching our conversation in sign language, said,

'Madam, please give her a guava that has been half-eaten by a parrot. Just stand near a guava tree for some time and wait till a parrot pecks at a fruit. Pluck it immediately and give it to your daughter to eat. I guarantee that she will start talking.'

CP of course refused to help me with the parrot and guava tree programme.

During our summer holidays in Coonoor, we passed a long stretch of forest. CP got down to click photographs and came back to find me in an excited discussion with the driver. I told him breathlessly, 'These forests have been cordoned off because the locals believe that there are medicinal plants here that can cure anything. To dissuade them from plucking mindlessly, the local government has put up barriers. But the driver knows a way to get in. If we go straight down the hillock and move strategically, there is a way we can enter the forest.'

CP gave the driver a singularly unfriendly look. '*Aap idea dene ke liye aaye hain, ki gaadi chalane ke liye*? (Are you here to give us ideas or drive the car?)'

Still, my mind used to race feverishly as known and unknown people contributed ideas to cure my children of their various ailments. Like millions of mothers before and after me, I carry hope like a candle that burns endlessly in my heart.

Jayashree has been profoundly uninterested in reading, though she is blessed with imagination. In one of our several attempts to get her to read and write, we asked her to write about the park next to our building. She presented an essay titled 'The Nameless Park'. It gave me the shivers. With three words, she stoked my imagination.

However, despite my effusive praise and hand-holding, she avoided books and read only *Those Dreadful Children* by Enid Blyton, which she had first read in Class II. To make matters worse, she would come to me at bedtime and say, 'Amma, I've finished one chapter of *Dreadful Children*. Can I go to sleep now?'

I pondered over the right book for her and invited her to complete twenty short stories from *The Room of Many Colours* by Ruskin Bond and discuss the storyline of each piece with me.

I was not very hopeful, but the author's easy style of writing, Jayashree says, makes her feel she is strolling down a lane, holding her Grandpa's hand and listening to his stories. When we discussed the first story, 'A Long Walk with Granny', she realised that people are not around forever. Her lips wobbled and she looked at me questioningly. I held on to my composure and told her, 'I may not be in the same room as you, Jayashree, but I can tell you that you will always be loved.'

The next day, Jayashree was unusually silent at dinnertime. When I finally made my way to the dinner table from the kitchen, I saw her with the book propped against a vessel as she ate her dinner.

Challenge met. A reader was born.

When CP returned home one evening, the watchman stopped him near the lift. '*Saab, ye aapki beti ne mujhe diya hai* (Sir, your daughter has given this to me),' he said, and dropped a gold earring into CP's palm.

Barely had CP entered the lift than Anil, our driver, breezed past. '*Arre saab, Lakshmi aaj gold earring deke gayi hai* (Hello sir, Lakshmi gave me her gold earring today).'

CP entered home with a strangely apoplectic air and headed straight for Lakshmi. She abandoned Shah Rukh Khan on the computer, and she and CP began a strange dance of a type that can probably be found on a yet-to-be-discovered island.

For every movement CP made, Lakshmi would move away and chant, 'Say sorry, say sorry,' with a distinctly unapologetic smile on her face. She won the round by her sheer gift for repetition.

The next occasion that warranted earrings saw us take Lakshmi to the jeweller. He regretfully informed us that the ears would have to be pierced again. That day, Lakshmi's lung power earned her a permanent place in the hall of fame of the Jewellers' Association of India.

This Diwali, my sister Vaidehi cracked the code. She picked up terracotta jhumkas, which I placed in the small mini department store we run at home that displays a variety of baubles, tubes and lotions. Lakshmi picked up the jhumkas and the rest was history.

Of course, stories of her largesse continue. When she tires of the jhumkas, she prises them off and says 'Take' to the nearest available person. However, the jhumkas cost one hundred rupees and Vaidehi has promised to keep us well supplied on a regular basis.

Once in a while, we find a jhumka in the car, in the breadbasket, with the watchman, by the computer. Lakshmi cobbles them together and wears them again when she feels like it.

She is a gypsy at heart, my Lakshmi.

Jayanthi throws both TV remotes down from our seventh-floor window. They land on the ledge below.

Breathing heavily, CP starts plotting a retrieval strategy.

Krishna says, 'Don't waste time. Buy a new remote.' CP gives him the standard response: 'You don't know the value of money.'

I make tea and get the kids to vamoose.

CP assembles a motley group of watchmen and others to hold a bedsheet along with him on the ground floor, strategically below the window.

I remind CP about the last time Jayanthi did this and make sure he takes a double bedsheet so that the remotes land appropriately.

Anil, our driver, self-appointed mentor and habitual tormentor, enters the scene, drinks CP's tea, and says, '*Yeh sab mat karo. Lamba lakdi lo, Fevikwik lagao, neeche utaaro aur remotes ko upar uthao. Bas* (Don't waste time. Just take a long stick, apply Fevikwik at the end, press it down on the remote and voila! The remote will come up).'

CP finds me laughing in the kitchen and gives me his patented look of icy disapproval.

Anil executes the Fevikwik plan with CP's unwilling assistance and manages to bring up only the stick sans remote. Anil hastily goes down to hold the bedsheet.

CP laboriously starts explaining to me the process of pushing the remotes down after he gives the signal from below. Our neighbour's son offers to take over. I move back to the kitchen.

Our young friend pushes the remotes down even before CP enters the elevator.

The motley group vanishes after handing the remnants of the remotes to CP in a garbage bag.

I make more tea.

Krishna says, 'See, I told you to buy a new remote.'

Once upon a time, long, long ago, we had a profusion of flowering plants on our terrace that were regularly tended to by our maali. One morning, I took him to task about why my plants were not growing at all. I think the poor man had been waiting to be asked and he gave me an aggrieved look.

'*Kaise badey honge aapke paudhe, aapki bachchi saara naya patta kha leti hai* (How will your plants grow? Your daughter eats up all the new leaves).'

Seeing my purplish countenance, Jayashree chimed in, 'Amma, you don't know? Jayanthi eats up all the new leaves every morning. Now she will come out of her room. Just see what happens.'

Sure enough, Jayanthi emerged dewy-eyed from her room, smiled gently at us and proceeded towards the terrace. We watched her with almost the same awe as once upon a time people watched

Gandhi-ji on his Dandi march. She wafted among the plants and proceeded to pop leaves into her mouth like Heidi's young goats.

Krishna, who has taken the 'Bhishma' vow of never consuming green vegetables unless they are served in kurkure packets, looked revolted, while Jayashree said, 'See, she is talking to the plants. They are her friends, Amma, that's why they are giving her their leaves.'

The maali looked vindicated and in need of counselling.

Jayanthi wafted off the terrace towards her earthly life.

I looked for CP. Like the maali, I was aggrieved. Why should I suffer alone?

Today, Jayanthi, after many sessions with me, has stopped eating the plants on the terrace, though her love for nature is still intense. We are planning to help her train to manage an organic garden. Who better than her to teach people to eat what they grow?

Once, I invited the kids to have a tête-à-tête with me. They asked me what that meant. I explained that I wanted a long chat with them. The next day, Jayashree of 'my teacher taughten me' fame asked me for a teddy chat. I was puzzled. She explained, 'You remember that long chat thing you were telling me about?'

That was it! The name stuck and it sounded more appealing too. Now, no day is complete without a 'teddy chat' at bedtime, surrounded by some two thousand pillows (since we have quadruplets, our lovely friends donate blankets, pillows and storybooks, not realising that I have storage issues).

The kids air their grievances. Jayashree says that her best friend is now someone else's best friend. Krishna, who is a voracious reader, asks me why Tim Cook is proud to be gay and we discuss the importance of respect and coexistence. Lakshmi busily tries to unscrew Jayashree's gold earrings and earns a glare from me. She shifts mode and starts singing bhajans extempore. CP pops in and sarcastically asks Krishna for permission to switch off the lights in his room. CP pauses and even he can't resist the tangle of pillows and the innocent faces of our children. He joins in and the teddy chat resumes.

The air conditioners in the house stopped working mysteriously. CP, who is justifiably proud of his ability to remedy most issues (he has been trained by us for so many years), could not figure out the problem. The AC mechanic came and opened the AC. He paused and gave us a bewildered look. Then he began removing a trove of things—small combs, clips, pens, pencils and my ruby earrings. He said, '*Madam, yeh sab aapko locker me rakhna chahiye. Nahi toh AC kaise kaam karega* (Madam, you should keep your valuables in your cupboard. How will the AC work otherwise)?'

The kids hastily held a conference and informed me that Jayanthi is being taught to keep things in their place. Whenever she is confused, she puts them in the AC.

What could I do? I made tea for the mechanic. He gave me a doubtful look before accepting it, then left with a confused look on his face.

The day we transitioned from feeding bottle to non-bottle intake was a red-letter day. We first packed all the bottles into a container and put them out of reach in the loft. This was to prevent me from weakening at the last moment and giving in to the bottle.

We also bought a variety of small and big garishly coloured glasses and spouts to motivate our brood to consume their milk from something other than a bottle. I strategically lined up a variety of toys, whistles (to outshout them if they yelled too much), and plenty of soft tissues to mop their faces with if they cried too much.

CP, thankfully, left for work corporate style, with, 'Let me know if you need my inputs' or some such nice, polite, rubbishy statement. Then, my elderly ayah and I settled down with the babies who were eagerly awaiting their morning feed.

Lakshmi gave a couple of yells, but as soon as she realised that she could actually control her intake from a glass and gobble up more, she grew blissful. We had to find a way to negotiate Krishna's tiny body and enormous head with the glass. It was fairly torturous, but like Lakshmi, he kind of settled on day one itself. Jayashree proved more militant and gave us nervous moments through the day. She refused to let us put the glass to her mouth. We had to let her go hungry a bit, quickly slip in a bit. This went on till day two. Jayanthi commanded the attention of the entire force. Me, the ayah, our helper, her sister who worked in the same building, our driver Anil bhaiya, his wife who he called agitatedly, all my immediate neighbours, my parents, CP's parents, everyone got to play a role. Jayanthi's gentle disposition and my implacability turned me into an instant life-size replica of Jim Corbett's man-eaters of Kumaon, a dubious reputation that I continue to enjoy to this day.

If you want people to know every detail about you, go to YouTube on your TV when there are visitors at home. It happened to me some time ago.

First, YouTube asks you to identify yourself. I clicked on 'Sangeetha'.

Everything I had searched for, watched and was in the process of watching was there for everybody to view.

Some showed me in a positive light: Debates in parliament.

Something culinary: How to make stuffed brinjal.

Something cultural: *Seetha Kalyanam* by M.S. Subbulakshmi.

Some that make Jayashree and Krishna say, 'We can't believe you actually watch these shows!': *Balika Vadhu. Bhagyalakshmi.*

Some that are aspirational: How to grow long and thick hair.

Some that show anxiety: How to make your hair look decent in a ponytail when you have lost a lot of hair but you want it to look like Dimple Kapadia's. (I last heard she washes her hair with eggs and beer. That will require quite some effort on my part. 'Pooja Stores? *Achcha, zara do litre beer bhej do* (Please send two litres of beer).'

Some that show desperation: How to lose weight in thirty days before the next doctor's appointment, without doing anything strenuous or stressful, while smiling and leading a peaceful life.

The TV has become a counsellor, far from the TV I had at home as a child. A black and white Dyanora, the eagerly anticipated Sunday movie, the weekly musical potluck *Chitrahaar* and the painfully orchestrated news programmes.

Then came the era of cable TV, and I remember the day the cablewala came home to give us the connection and we looked at him with the same awe that would be on our faces if Bill Gates walked in to install Microsoft for us.

The most bewildering is the Smart TV where I have to go through multiple steps to arrive at what I want. Jayashree and Krishna are my unpaid, overworked assistants and have made a checklist for me.

Amazon Prime: Rajinikanth, Neena Gupta, Vyjayanthimala, Meena Kumari movies.

Sony Max: Agatha Christie.

YouTube: How to look intelligent when you receive a Taj Experience Gift Hamper with avocado oil, Welsh cheddar and festive table settings with runner. (CP: 'What is runner, Sangeetha?' Me: 'It's that long thing that you put on the dining table when you have matching cutlery and don't dump all the spoons in an old coffee mug, while secretly wishing that someone had gifted you Sunrise coffee and sturdy coffee mugs that don't break easily.')

Netflix: For those under sixteen years old. 'Amma, people don't use pure English all the time like you. You watch TV in the living room and when the shows get too colourful, the rest of us feel awkward around you. Better you watch shows and movies for those over thirteen years old, like *Home Alone, Animal Babies* and *Lonely Planet*.'

———◦◉◦———

We are at Srivilliputhur, the seat of the young saint Andal, one of the most ancient and celebrated temples in Tamil Nadu.

Jayanthi was being given medication in the form of tablets for the first time. I tried pushing one down her throat but she smiled and brought it out. I popped in the tablet again and poured some water into her mouth. She smiled, made the sign for brushing the teeth, and spat the water out in a most ladylike manner. I considered waking up CP, who was in slumberland, to ask him to activate 'The Look'.

Jayashree came to the rescue. She said, 'Amma, how many tablets?'

I said, 'Three.'

She said, 'Amma, just say, "Jayanthi, take Mentos" and give them to her. She will take them herself.'

I looked at her doubtfully, but Jayashree was supremely confident.

Feeling slightly foolish, I gave Jayanthi the tablets and said, 'Jayanthi, take Mentos.' She smiled, popped them into her mouth one by one and swallowed them. I gave her some water. She drank it.

We went to bed.

———◦◉◦———

Jayashree and I were arguing about who knows Krishna better. I said, 'He was in my tummy for eight and a half months. I know him better.' Jayashree chimed in, 'He was in your tummy for eight and a half months, but I was his neighbour. You were outside, but I was talking to him the whole time.'

This morning, I took a well-deserved break from idlis and dosas and dispensed a breakfast of Nutella sandwiches. Jayashree said, 'Amma, don't put butter in Jayanthi's sandwiches.'

I asked why. She said, 'Because I don't like butter. So she also won't like it. Just see! She will eat faster now.'

One day, these children will realise that they will have to walk different paths. That day will be the end of innocence. But I hope they remain united by their love for each other, wherever they may be.

CP waits for someone in the family to fall ill. He administers his home remedies with a charming air of, 'Do what I say or perish,' which is impossible to resist.

When I returned from surgery, he unveiled the monster pillow: a huge slanting contraption against which one can lie upright and yet at an incline.

'What is this!' I gasped. 'Horrible!'

The children giggled as CP said, 'I've just bought it for Rs 2,000. Please use it.'

If by chance one of us rubs our eyes and says, 'My eyes are burning. I want to sleep', out comes the bottle of Refresh eye drops. What I find daunting is the way CP pries open the eye in seconds and puts in the drops. With Lakshmi and Jayanthi, it works brilliantly. Before they know what's happening, it's done. Jayashree complains vigorously, but only after her eye has been pried open and the drops have been put in. Krishna is very smart. He shifted from Mumbai to Bangalore. As for me, I sidle away, chanting, 'Give it to me. I will do it. Give it to me. I will do it', with CP in hot pursuit.

After this unseemly struggle, the drops are finally administered.

The one battle he has not won is in the kitchen. Tired of seeing the milk spill over every morning, he bought a milk cooker—a noisy, water-spilling contraption.

I watched curiously as he demonstrated its use. CP and I were in the kitchen and so was Urmila didi, whose main task is to wander from room to room, looking busy.

I was washing my puja vessels. Urmila was making the only thing she knows how to make—ginger tea.

The milk cooker sat on the gas stove and CP looked on proudly.

After some time, as I rinsed the puja vessels, I heard a low hissing sound, as if ten to twelve snakes were about to make their presence felt.

I looked at the milk cooker. CP appeared unconcerned.

Then the hissing escalated and a few drops of scalding water flew from the cooker in all directions.

CP's ears turned a mild pink, I stood and watched the cooker, Urmila asked, 'Yeh shout kyun kar raha hai (Why is this shouting)?'

CP, of course, did not reply.

Then the milk cooker began to whistle in earnest and small horizontal waterfalls erupted from both its sides.

I could not contain my mirth. CP retained the grave demeanour that he has probably worn since the cradle. He avoided looking at me and did not answer Urmila's voluble questions.

It was a victory of sorts for CP because the milk cooker, with its sheer noise power, makes its presence felt and so the milk never boils over.

I too won. How? When it was my turn to make coffee, the milk cooker started the nagin dance again. I waited for CP to leave the kitchen. Then I transferred the milk from the milk cooker to another vessel and heated it.

Added two teaspoons of Sunrise, half a tablet of Sugar Free, a quarter cup of boiling water. Poured from one glass to another till mixed and a heavenly fragrance emanated. Poured very little scalding hot milk into it. Looked at it approvingly.

Took it to Sai Baba. 'Krishnarpanam (Whatever I have, I offer you, Krishna).'

Just as I started drinking the coffee, CP returned to the kitchen and looked disapprovingly at my subterfuge.

Then, it was Urmila's turn to make tea. She is more loyal to CP. She glanced here and there. '*Sir ka shouting bartan kahan hai* (Where is sir's shouting vessel)?'

I remember the day Jayanthi was diagnosed with autism. Just two years old, she sat next to me in the car. We were on our way to Ummeed Child Development Centre. My heart was thumping. I could barely focus when the driver asked me where we were to go. I just wanted to get to Ummeed and convince them that the strange sounds that Jayanthi made, the way she lifted her hands to her face to stare at her fingers, her complete focus on herself, her lack of response to her name, were not of any significance.

I felt a wave of embarrassment as the driver turned to look at Jayanthi due to the sounds she was making, and I tried to get her to stop.

This was my first step into autism parenting. The beginning is traumatic, socially debilitating and takes a toll on every relationship. The parent cringes when his child is the painfully odd one out at a party. When the parent can't make a simple introduction to his friends, 'This is my son, Gaurav', because he knows Gaurav will be looking on blankly. At a family wedding, his child is the only one who does not mingle with his cousins. He uses the bathroom with the door open even at other people's homes. Every awkward behaviour, every strange sound, every anomaly grates on the feelings of a new autism parent.

The embarrassment is acute, the hurt deep and the smile plastic. Parties are endured rather than enjoyed as the parent deals with a child who, through his behaviour, announces to the world: I am not the same as you.

With the passage of time, the parent's hurt is washed away by the child's innocence. Her despondence is converted to courage when she sees her child slowly learning. Rays of hope fill her heart as she sees her child draw or paint or dance or sing.

A new resolve strengthens her shoulders as she starts reading about autism, attending workshops and learning ways to decode her child.

The same parent calmly tells Jayanthi as she hums loudly in an elevator full of people, 'Jayanthi, quiet time.'

She stands outside the washroom in a mall with no discomfort at all and clearly instructs Jayanthi, 'Please lock the door. Do you need help?'

She smilingly approaches her host at a party. 'Jayanthi and I will sit in that quiet corner. Is that okay?'

The same parent firmly tells Gaurav as he decides to masturbate in a mall, 'Gaurav, please go to the bathroom, not here', and waits for him to stop and escorts him to the bathroom.

She uses all her understanding and reflexes when Gaurav starts weeping at a family wedding and wants to go home that very moment. She calmly apologises and leaves with her son.

She goes home, helps her child unwind, makes herself a drink of cocoa or Thums Up or wine before hitting the bed. Yet again, before her head touches the pillow, she makes her way to her sleeping child who is no longer a child. Looks at his wan face, puts her hand over his locks of hair, presses her lips to his forehead, sheds quiet tears for their shared journey that is sometimes full of hope and sometimes undetermined, sometimes charged with achievement and sometimes confused and irresolute.

Another day begins the next morning. She picks up her phone and starts typing on her parent WhatsApp group, 'I had a problem with Rahul at a party last night.' She sends an email to her child's therapist, 'Rahul needs help.' She calls up Forum for Autism, 'I am an autism parent. Can I get a counsellor? I need to talk.'

―――◆◉◆―――

Three weeks ago, Jayashree told me that she would travel alone by auto to Dharmakshetra, the Sai Baba temple that is a ten- to twelve-minute ride from our place.

I baulked and asked, 'Why don't you go with Krishna?'

'Why?'

'Because ... er... It's better, isn't it? Two people instead of one.'

'But you never tell Krishna this when he goes to Dharmakshetra. In fact, he goes to Bandra by auto on his own.'

Then, she attacked a little more minutely.

'What happened, Amma. You don't trust me?'

I answered with what I felt was a masterstroke.

'Of course I trust you, Jayashree. It's just that I don't trust the auto driver.'

Jayashree parried back, 'What do you think the auto fellow will do?'

I said, 'Let's not get into it. There are many things people do, Jayashree, that breach a person's body, mind, soul and right to dignity. I have discussed safety with you. You know what I am talking about.'

'Okay. If the auto driver does try to hurt me in some way, what do you think Krishna will do that I can't?'

I felt so small then. On the one hand, there was my open anxiety and fear for my fourteen-year-old daughter's welfare and on the other, my belief that she should live with confidence, poise and human values.

'I am sorry, Jayashree. You are right, but I am scared. Please bear with me. Okay, go to Dharmakshetra on your own. Please call me once you get there. Click a picture of the auto number on your mobile and WhatsApp me. Make sure the auto driver sees you doing it.'

After ten minutes, she called. Her voice was pulsating with pride and excitement. 'Thank you, Amma,' she said.

We are in Tirupati, a hastily planned and executed trip. We own around seven suitcases and six overnight bags in total. This I am sharing with the disclaimer that neither CP nor I will win any prize as far as style goes. This time, I decided that each person would take one suitcase and manage it during the entire trip.

We have not bought suitcases since the kids were born and therefore, some have a distinctly medieval appearance. I got the largest, since all extras are stashed in mine. Jayanthi got the next in size since she believes in changing clothes three times a day. Lakshmi and Jayashree got regular small size suitcases. CP, who believes in minimalism, had an unnaturally low number of clothes and other stuff in a separate bag.

This was when we realised that there was nothing for Krishna. Since he was not around to fight for his rights, CP and I pulled out something that looked suspiciously like a briefcase that once my father must have carried to work.

A captivating and unusual colour between grey and cream, it shook slightly when we picked it up but manfully accommodated Krishna's clothes. Its handles were winsome and charming, reminding you of the visuals in history textbooks of some forgotten dynasty.

Our helper came in after all the work was done and put the suitcases neatly in line for us, but left Krishna's behind. I shouted from the kitchen, '*Woh bhi lena* (Take that one too).'

She looked concerned. '*Yeh wala ... maine socha raddi paper ke liye rakhenge* (This one? I thought was for storing old newspapers).'

I glared and said, 'Please, Urmila, *aap advice mat karo* (Please don't advise me, Urmila).'

I think Krishna got a clear view of his suitcase only when it was being loaded into the car. The look he gave us was a fine amalgamation of outrage, horror and lack of filial respect. Both CP and I looked sympathetic and helpful. I tried to boost his morale. 'You are the eldest, Krishna. You have to lead from the front and adjust in a tough situation.'

The finale took place at the airport. The luggage handler, while tossing in our baggage, took one look at Krishna's. He paused and brought out a brown rope-like thing of the kind that is used to secure gunny bags in kirana shops. He bound it tightly around the suitcase before tossing it in. We all watched with respect as it moved slowly down the conveyor belt, bearing strong testimony to the Chakrapani family's unique style of 'Can do. Will do.'

This morning is the last of our three-day stay at Tirumala, Tirupati.

Day 1, 6 p.m.: We were outside the temple where vendors were selling freshly prepared snacks. All of us chose steamed corn and I anxiously scouted for an alternative for Jayanthi who does not chew well. I saw fresh bondas (round, soft vadas) and persuaded CP to buy them for Jayanthi. They were outstandingly delicious! Jayanthi fell on them and gobbled them up, allowing the rest of us to taste one piece.

Inside the temple, throngs of devotees had settled themselves in different parts of the huge courtyard. We walked on the stone-flagged pathways, taking in the sights and sharing Jayanthi's enthusiasm for jumping down the big stone steps. Lakshmi held Krishna's hand tightly and chanted 'Sai' throughout her temple visit.

Day 2, evening: We made our way to the bonda stall and ordered individual plates for each of us. The bonda-seller was not surprised and smilingly served us. All of us wolfed down our bondas and then entered the temple for a long walk. The stone-laid pathways felt cool and comforting beneath our feet. Queues of devotees, who had been waiting hours for darshan, were chanting, 'Govinda, Govinda', to keep their morale up. We saw many balloon-sellers with bunches of small balloons fixed onto an elongated balloon. My childhood memories came rushing back and I asked CP to get me a balloon. He was amazed but obliged immediately. The kids, particularly Lakshmi, joined in the fun. Clutching one balloon each, we made our way back.

On our last evening there, we made our last visit to the bonda-seller. It was our last treat before going home. The bonda-seller gave Jayanthi the first plate. We took a picture of him before taking leave and waving him goodbye.

We reached the end of our walk and sat down for ten minutes before leaving the temple. All of us were silent till Krishna said, 'We have to go back tomorrow.' There was so much more left unsaid in his words.

The simple act of walking together as a family without any great agenda had been so fulfilling for all of us. We had shared so much, casually chatting, arguing with, and laughing at, each other. I told CP that it would be great if we managed this even once a week in Mumbai. Tall order! Our schedules will consume us once we are back. Maybe we will do it. Maybe we won't. But the magic of walking together will stay with us.

Do you remember the Woodward's Gripe Water advertisement?

The mother asks her daughter, '*Kya hua* (What happened)?'

The daughter says, '*Bachchi roh rahi thi* (The baby is crying).'

The mother replies, 'Woodward's *de de. Wohi toh mein deti thi jab tum chhoti thi* (Give her Woodward's. That's what I gave you when you were a baby).'

This mother's mother asks, '*Kya hua?*'

The mother replies, '*Bachchi roh rahi thi.*'

Full of wisdom, the grandmother replies, 'Woodward's *de de. Wohi toh mein deti thi jab tum chhoti thi.*'

Similarly, young and old parents give precious, precious words of reassurance to this mother: 'Don't worry. This too shall pass.'

Autism parenting. The beginning is sharp and painful. This is the time for everyone around to envelope the parent in comfort. This is the time for everyone around to become a Woodward's Gripe Water mother.

Lakshmi was three years old. She had just been diagnosed with autism. Jayanthi had been diagnosed a year earlier.

Lakshmi would come out in the morning after a night's sleep and the whole house would be on edge. Why? Lakshmi's Bournvita had to be ready and placed on the table. If her milk was not ready, she would start howling and shrieking, roll on the floor, and finally throw up in her agitation. This would happen if there was even a one-minute delay in giving her a glass of Bournvita.

I knew there was something very wrong in the way the entire family was pandering to Lakshmi's tantrums. I had a meeting with CP, our helpers and extended family members to make sure absolutely nobody interfered with me.

At 4 p.m., Lakshmi came out after her nap. Cute as a button, it was almost impossible to resist her. I called out, 'Lakshmi, wait. I will give you your milk.'

Her face turned red and she threw a world-class tantrum of dizzying proportions.

I started boiling the milk, cooled it a bit, and added Bournvita. This took three minutes. All the other family members went about their work. The other kids watched in wide-eyed wonder.

I brought Lakshmi's Bournvita to the table: 'Lakshmi, drink your milk.' I kept the glass within easy reach and settled down close by.

The others drank their Bournvita. Lakshmi refused to touch hers. The milk went cold. She went hungry till around 6 p.m. and then ate a small banana.

The next morning, at 7 a.m., I did the same thing. This time Lakshmi howled. Then she drank the milk and threw up. I helped her get cleaned up and put her on my lap for some time.

At 4 p.m. the same day, Lakshmi drank her milk without a fuss.

We clapped for her and broke into a war dance.

I had a problem with the way we used to tiptoe around Lakshmi. I had visions of her demanding her birthright in the form of food, what exactly to wear, where exactly to sleep. The Bournvita behaviour could have reached monstrous proportions in all areas of Lakshmi's life, making it difficult for her to coexist with her parents, teachers, extended family members and caregivers.

Over the years, I faced challenges with both Lakshmi and Jayanthi on a daily basis. I still do, but constantly negotiate to help them understand that life is not a monarchy and they are not kings. It is a democracy and they need to be able to give and take.

For every tear I shed, I march one step forward.

There are not enough words in the dictionary, there is not enough balm in the world, there is no amount of reassurance available to assuage the anxiety of an autism parent.

When you see your grown child sleeping blissfully, so secure in the faith that his parents will take care of him. When you sit by the side of your child in the early hours of the morning and try to stop your mind from wandering too much into the future.

When you get emotional about something silly like:

How will people understand that he loves palak only in palak paneer?

He eats idli only in restaurants but not at home.

He is independent in the washroom but someone has to ensure that he has soap, toothpaste, etc.

He gargles after brushing, but needs a glass to pour water into his mouth.

He speaks, but so little and it's all unclear, so it takes a while to understand what he is saying.

He does not speak at all, but he points, but he takes time to point. Who will have the patience to wait, to try and understand what he is trying to say?

Your heart explodes with grief when you realise that you may not celebrate his fiftieth birthday with him. Who will surround him with love and celebrate his birthday with pride and joy when you are not around?

Who will tick him off for not behaving properly or be firm with him when he is going into damage mode? Who will go into his room hours after ticking him off and make up with him? Who will reassure him that, 'I know I am tough with you, but I love you and I am there for you and I understand you and we are going to be alright'?

Sometimes, the cauldron of feelings in the heart has no space for expression. Your spouse, your friends, your mother ... nobody can absorb this anxiety.

The umbilical cord extends into every part of the human body. The fact that it is cut at birth is a scientific joke and has no connection with reality.

However, this umbilical cord has so much strength. It has the strength to help us look into the future resolutely, to plan an independent life for our children, to let them go. At such times, despite all the anxiety we experience for the unknown future that awaits our children, it is our faith in them, their capacity to cope with the vagaries of life, their innate abilities rather than their disability, that helps us march forward.

For every tear I shed, I will march one step forward.

Every single auto refused me when I wanted to go to Holy Spirit Hospital for a physio appointment.

Running out of time, I requested the last auto driver to increase his fare and take me. He said, 'No need. Get in.'

'Wait,' I told the auto driver and fell into deep reflection over how to enter the auto.

Should I dump my bags inside, hold the little railing on top and heave myself inside?

Should I hold both sides of the auto, take a deep breath, invoke the spirit of Bahubali and seat myself?

Should I invoke the spirit of Alia Bhatt and try a more graceful and womanly entry by sliding in sideways, somehow manipulating my thirty excess kilos?

Never mind. I somehow entered the auto and the driver looked as relieved as I felt.

The first and last question I asked the auto driver was, '*Bhaiya, aap GPay lete hain* (Do you accept GPay)?'

'*Madam, ye duniya aisi hai* (This world is a difficult place).'

I blinked.

'*Sab fayda uthate hain. Sab kamine hain* (Everywhere, there are villains ready to loot you).'

I sought to improve my ratings with him. Surely he did not think I was trying to hoodwink him?

'*Bhaiya, koi baat nahin* (It doesn't matter),' I tried to say, but the driver was in full flood.

I was struck by his uncharitable view on everything. How dismal he is, I thought to myself.

He talked about his wife and his grievances with his kids, evidently seeing me as his on-the-spot, captive counsellor.

I got out of the auto with considerably greater dexterity than I had got in and the driver finally answered my question.

'Thirty rupees,' he said.

No, he did not accept GPay.

'Oh!'

I scrabbled around in my bag. Like Mukesh Ambani, Warren Buffett and other prosperous people, I don't carry cash. However, unlike Ambani, whose story of borrowing money from a fellow passenger was carried in newspapers across the world, nobody has ever been remotely excited by the fact that CP and I borrow money from our driver, Anil bhaiya, every day. Every few days, Anil politely sends us a message about his dues and after several meaningful nods to each other—'You transfer,' 'No, you transfer'—one of us finally transfers the amount via GPay to Anil.

That morning, Anil was not around to bail me out.

My auto driver, who had bemoaned the 'zaalim zamana (evil world)', was himself so gracious.

Not a frown or glimmer of irritation. He just waved me away!

'*Koi baat nahin, aap jao* (It's okay. Go)!'

'*Par aapke paise* (What about your money)?'

'*Arre madam, jaane do* (Never mind, let it go),' he said, and he swivelled his auto around.

Like a Hindi movie, where the happy ending appears from nowhere, my hand landed on a crumpled fifty-rupee note in my bag.

'Auto bhaiya,' I shouted, and ponderously moved after the auto.

Fortunately, my voice travelled faster than my body and auto bhaiya peeped out.

'*Yeh lijiye* (Here, take this).'

His hand closed around the note and his toothy smile lit up the dark interior of his auto as he drove away.

We have a beautiful, massive fridge. It is the love of my life.

Lakshmi loves the fridge even more than I do and her incessant drinking of ice-cold water throughout the day resulted in long periods of coughs and colds.

Strategy 1

I shifted the water bottles to the vegetable compartment.
  She found them.

Strategy 2

I hid the bottles behind the giant idli batter vessels in the fridge.
  She found them.

Strategy 3

I kept a couple of bottles in the freezer and none in the fridge.
  She moved the ones outside into the fridge.

Strategy 4

With a heavy heart I stopped stocking water bottles in the fridge.

This turned out to be a temporary victory that lasted around a week.

She started filling bottles and putting them in the fridge.

Strategy 5

I went into deep meditation. I called on all the gods, devis, devtas, and realised that it is not possible to stand guard over the fridge all the time.

Strategy 6

Question: What does Lakshmi want?

Answer: Water from the fridge.

Question: Is she very particular that it should be ice-cold?

Answer: I don't think so.

Question: Even if she is very particular, if the fridge does not produce ice-cold water, can Lakshmi do anything about it?

Answer: No, unless she interns with Samsung Refrigerators.

So, for the past two days, I have been keeping four bottles of water in the fridge and six bottles of water outside.

Every two hours, I take out the four bottles from the fridge and replace them with the ones outside. I make my last switch at 11 p.m., after which my duties to the Chakrapani household end till 5.30 a.m. the next morning.

Lakshmi is happy that the fridge is stocked.

I am happy that I am smarter than Lakshmi.

For parents, there is no bigger proof of kids becoming teenagers than the simple sentence, 'Close the door.'

Jayashree started the movement at home. We can't complain because she is in Class X and it is the fundamental right, enshrined in the Constitution, for Class X children to only study.

Krishna is more gentlemanly and says it with a slightly apologetic touch. 'Do close the door', or something like that.

The problem is that this is a home, not the Four Seasons hotel (not that we could claim to be the Four Seasons in any case. I mean, which self-respecting hotel would use buckets to store clothes, not to mention the fact that our cushion covers have the look of Holi clothes after Holi has been played).

This is a home and when CP or I open a door to take something from the kids' rooms, they look up with an enquiring air that indirectly says, 'What are YOU doing HERE?'

CP and I are, however, manufactured from very tough material that rivals the gunny sacks in which potatoes are stored the whole year. So we breeze in. Barely have our feet touched the threshold of the room than the words emerge: 'Close the door.'

CP, of course, emits a dangerous aura that needs no words. Lucky man. I don't know from what tender age he has been practising this look. The kids don't say those three words very forcefully. They bleat them out.

With me, it is a short, crisp instruction.

Lakshmi has also joined this hallowed gallery. She takes things to a more universal level. Her deal is, 'When I listen to music, I need to be alone.'

So what she does is broken into three parts:

1. She physically propels people out. All of us, except CP whom she tolerates.
2. She shuts the door.
3. If you resist, she says crisply, 'Shut up', and while you are struggling to digest the insult, she quickly pushes you out.

Jayanthi came out from my womb but actually emerged from Lumbini Garden at Bodh Gaya.

For Jayanthi, the door does not exist. She belongs to everyone. Everyone belongs to her. She is the air, the trees, the leaves on the trees, the birds on the trees. She is a part of the universe. The universe is her.

How would you feel if a close family friend comes home one day, sits next to you, and asks you, 'What is your name?'

To this, your mother or father encourages you, 'Tell uncle your name ... tell ... tell.'

Ludicrous, is it not?

This happens often to people with autism.

They are quiet by nature. They don't feel the burning need to look at you, to talk to you. They don't assess your clothes and mentally compare them with what anyone else is wearing. They don't want to know how much you are earning or whether the red stones in your ears are rubies. And they don't want to know what was the last movie you watched.

People with autism communicate in a very subtle and individual way. However, their silence and quietness are often prodded in ways that are not dignified, meaningful or age appropriate.

For example, Tina has autism. She is twenty-two years old. She works at a shop. She has got back home after a long day at work. She is sitting at the table quietly.

Rahul is Tina's uncle. Tina's sheer quietness is daunting to Rahul. He has to DO something about it.

So he looks at her KINDLY and asks, 'So, what is your name?'

Imagine! This is a conversation starter by a neurotypical person towards a person with autism, a person he has known since childhood.

Tina is the picture of dignity and does not reply. Neither does she look at Rahul. She continues doing what she is doing until Rahul repeats the question insistently.

Tina looks up blankly. She may or may not reply.

At this point, Tina's mother or guardian has two choices.

Option 1

The avoidable choice: 'Tina, tell uncle your name. Tell him, "My name is Tina."'

Tina finally responds to this sustained and totally unnecessary intrusion and mumbles her name.

'Wow, very good,' Rahul says. 'How nicely she is saying her name!'

Option 2

Tina's mother gently intervenes. 'Hey, Rahul, surely you know Tina's name.'

Then Tina's mother assesses her daughter's mood and suggests any of the following:

1. 'Rahul, would you like to join me and Tina for a game of carrom?'
2. 'Rahul, this is when Tina likes to go for a walk. We can walk with her.'
3. 'Rahul, this is Tina's quiet time. Why don't we all have a game of carrom after dinner?'
4. 'Rahul, let me show you a video of Tina at her workplace. You can really bond with her by doing some activities that she likes to do.'

By this gentle and firm intervention, Tina gets her space, dignity and chance to be understood as a person. By this intervention, Rahul understands that it is perfectly okay to sit quietly with a person with autism. He does not have to engage the person with talk. He does not have to feel guilty that he has not tried.

The Rahuls of the world feel guilty and bewildered and pained by a Tina whom they don't understand and don't know how to approach.

Through this intervention, Rahul understands the beauty of interaction with a person with autism.

Rule 1: Don't ask questions. And if you must, ask age-appropriate questions. People with autism find it tough to process and answer the simplest of questions, which is not a reflection on their knowledge or abilities.

Rule 2: Find a way to bond that engages a person with autism in a comfortable and familiar space. It could be something simple like shelling peas, or going for a walk, or looking outside the window.

Rule 3: Be, and let Tina be.

I am not an organised homemaker. Organised homemakers are those who have pre-ordered grocery lists and never need to frantically order ginger when the water is bubbling on the stove or rava when all the veggies are cut and ready for vegetable upma or even worse, basics like salt.

I have ongoing research at any point of time for grocery apps that deliver fast, preferably with free delivery. At this point in time, Swiggy Instamart would deliver in twenty-five minutes and charged up to fifty rupees for delivery.

I've now become a fan of Blinkit, which was earlier known as Grofers. They deliver in eight minutes. Eight! And there's free delivery!

CP asked me, full of his trademark sarcastic wisdom, if they will also come home and make the upma.

'I don't mind,' I replied. 'But you definitely will.'

Sometimes, humility is not a virtue. Both CP and my father know that my upma and my chutney occupy a heavenly category and that I should ideally be presiding over the kitchens of the Taj or the JW Marriot instead of that at my home in Poonam Nagar, Andheri East.

As I scroll through Blinkit, I notice a WhatsApp message flash from Super Store, Andheri.

I think, why not order from them?

Then I hesitate. If I order from Super Store, I will have to call up and TALK!

The app does not need me to talk, to interact. In seconds, I tap a few buttons and am done.

Is this not what many prefer to do these days?

WhatsApp has reinvented relationship building.

The birth of a baby, a much-anticipated promotion at work, a medical emergency, the loss of a loved one ...

In the closest of relationships, the lilt of our voice, the gurgle of laughter from our throat, the catch of anxiety in our tone and quiet sobbing on the phone have been replaced by WhatsApp.

I go to Super Store. The shopkeeper is busy organising his shelves.

'*Arre bhabhi-ji, kya doon aapko* (Hello, what can I give you)?'

'*Yeh khakhra leti hoon* (I will take the khakhra).'

My phone rings, I take the call and as I talk, he points to the things I usually order. I nod when I see what I want. Then just as I am about to leave, he says, 'Wait!' and gives me a small packet of flavoured coconut powder.

'*Aapko rice sevai ke saath kaam aayega* (This will be useful when you make rice sevai).'

I thank him as both of us rue that Concorde has stopped selling seasoning packets with their rice sevai.

He waves away my request for the bill.

'*Mera ladka aapko WhatsApp karega, aap jao. GPay kar do* (My boy will send you the bill on WhatsApp. You can GPay).'

Again, he stops me before I leave. '*Ek saal ke baad aap samaan le rahe ho* (You are buying from us after more than a year).'

This time I pause.

'*Bhaiya, aage se WhatsApp kar doongi* (I will WhatsApp my order to you from now on).'

'Okay ji.'

While we keep finding more ways to save time in order to accomplish more things, a visit to a store in the locality, a shopkeeper who knows your family, the vegetable vendor who knows you buy Bangalore tomatoes, the fruit-seller who calls and tells you, '*Kinu oranges hain, bhej doon* (Kinu oranges have come. Shall I send some to you)?' are human connections who enrich our lives.

I feel a sense of deprivation to think of a day when I go to the market and see a sea of unknown faces and not get the comfort of, '*Bhabhi-ji, Mahabaleshwar ke strawberries aaye hain. Ladka ke saath bhej deta hoon shaam ko* (Fresh strawberries have come in from Mahabaleshwar. I will send some to your house with my boy in the evening).'

———⊷⊙⊶———

I had a free lesson in Mumbai etiquette from Krishna one evening. The Christmas party at the Together Foundation had been simple and joyous. The tattoo artist had been a great hit and had patiently waited as the teachers and I googled our own unique Christmas designs. The bonhomie and sense of belonging was unmistakable.

Krishna came up to me. 'Amma, what are you doing?'

'I am waiting to get my tattoo done.'

'But where is tattoo uncle?'

I winced and glared.

'Why "uncle"?' I enquired icily.

'Okay, where is the tattoo wala?' came the reply.

Jayashree burst out laughing, Krishna was smiling easily, and I glared even more.

'Chill, Amma. Sometimes grammar does not matter.'

He was right. The tag of 'tattoo wala' would have been horribly impersonal.

So our driver is Anil bhaiya. The woman who comes to do the dishes is Neela mausi. Our house cleaner is Renuka didi. We have a 'lost and found section' lady who generally helps our family members present a civilised, cultured front to the world by tracing lunch dabbas, hairbrushes, phone chargers, pens, ID cards, clothes, bags, mobile phones and other critical possessions; we call her Urmila didi.

The kids have grown now. At the same time, they don't take the liberty of addressing helpers who are far older than them by name.

The other day, my neighbour sent her helper, Deepali, over to collect something. Jayashree went up to call her and said, '*Aap please kitchen mein aa jaiye* (Please come to the kitchen).'

I loved the courtesy she extended, while avoiding the didi tag. The kids are sixteen years old and learning to negotiate their way with people in the community, with courtesy.

The 'tattoo uncle' vs 'tattoo wala' episode shows that the kids have indeed grown up, and that they and are raising me as much as I am raising them.

Do you remember Kareena Kapoor's iconic dance on snow-crusted roads in the song *Yeh Ishq Hai* from the Hindi movie *Jab We Met*? Shahid Kapoor admiringly drives an open-air vehicle. When we went to the location of the dance, the snow did not look anything like the fluffy white snow in the movie.

I was wearing two layers of shawls and a monkey cap. As the children slept in the car, they huddled together in one mass that finally found its way to me such that I had one child resting her head against my shoulder, one sleeping on my lap, one resting her head against the one resting her shoulder against me, and one sleeping on top of the one sleeping on top of me.

CP was busily plotting where the family could stop for a bathroom break, after which his foremost duty was to check if the place was clean and then escort the kids there while I gave non-stop instructions.

'Make sure it's not an Indian loo.'

'Tell her to lock the door.'

'Stand outside the door, please.'

'Are you carrying the sanitiser? Please give it to her when she comes out.'

'Send her back to me. Take the next one.'

'Is there a shop where we can buy biscuit packets? No? So odd.'

'Please open the dicky. Under the orange bag, there is a green bag. In the side compartment, there is a ziplock packet with chips and biscuits.'

'How many hours left to get there? That long?'

'Where can we get tea?'

In the midst of this, the driver informed me that this was the road where Kareena Kapoor's song in *Jab We Met* was shot.

Our next tryst with Kareena Kapoor was Pangong Lake. The journey from the hotel to the lake was bumpy and torturous. I had ensured that the kids travelled on empty stomachs, to prevent nausea. When we got there, we tottered out of the car like a family of drunken bees.

In the far distance, I spied a few chairs and wearily made my way towards them, closely tailed by my brood.

This is where I realised that, except for the minor difference in physical appearance, our family has a past life connection with Kareena Kapoor.

When I reached the chairs, I blinked. They were shaped like the posterior of a human being and in lurid colours. I could not care less and sat down in one. The kids followed. By the time CP reached, there were no chairs left. All he had to do was pay money.

'Two hundred rupees per bum chair,' we were told.

Ignoring the uncivil description, I continued to sit in the contraption and asked, 'For sale?'

CP looked at me and the bum chair owner with a dangerous light in his eyes and demanded, 'Two hundred rupees each, er … each?'

'Haan ji, each bum chair for thirty minutes.'

'Kyun?'

'*Yeh Kareena wala hai* (These are the Kareena type of chairs).'

'Kareena? Kya? Kaun?'

CP, who finds it difficult to recognise any actors who don't appear on KTV and Sun TV, could not make the connection.

Still ensconced in the bum chair, I butted into the conversation uninvited.

'CP, these are the same chairs as the ones used in *3 Idiots*. That's why he is charging so much. Kareena Kapoor and Aamir Khan must have sat in these chairs.'

Saying this, I stroked my chair affectionately and hopefully, feeling that maybe a part of their glamorous genes would be transferred to me in that moment.

'*Do minute baaki hain. Wapas do sau dena padega into paanch— hazaar* (You have two minutes left, after which you'll have to pay me Rs 200 into five again, which is Rs 1,000),' said the attendant.

'Will you kindly get up?'

The five of us obliged, CP looked grateful that the Rs 1,000 did not become Rs 2,000 and we made our way around the lake where we could see Kareena's red scooter. This was Rs 500 rupees each to sit on and take a picture. All five of us kept a respectful distance from the scooter and obediently followed CP to the car.

As I got into the car and got into my shawls, I asked CP, 'Is there a loo here?'

'Yes, I've checked it out. I've also taken out the ziplock packet with biscuit packets from the side pocket of the green bag, which was under the orange bag.'

'When did you accomplish all this?' I asked admiringly.

'When we went to the lake and you escorted the children to the Rs 200 chairs.'

Do you remember that moment in school when you could not give the right answer immediately? Before you could try one more time, the teacher patted you kindly on the shoulder. 'Never mind, next time, okay?'

The frustration! I needed only one minute longer!

This is what happens frequently to many people with autism and their families.

A family is out with their son, Rohit, who has autism. They meet a good friend.

'Wow! What a surprise to see all of you here!'

A big round of hellos follows.

Mom: 'Rohit, look who's here! Sheena!'

Sheena: 'Hi, Rohit.'

Mom: 'Rohit, say hello to Sheena.'

Sheena: 'Hi, Rohit, hi!'

Dad: 'Rohit, Sheena is saying hi to you.'

Sheena: 'It's okay!'

Sheena pats Rohit on head or shoulder or some other available body part.

A big round of byes follows.

In this melee of conversation, Rohit did not get a chance to say hello and Sheena did not get a chance to connect with Rohit.

Situation 2

'Wow! Imagine meeting you here!'

'Hello! Hi! How are you doing?'

Sheena: 'Hello, Rohit!'

Pause.

Mom: 'Rohit, let's say hi to Sheena.'

Sheena: 'I also like talking with you, Rohit!'

Pause.

Pause.

Pause.

Pause for a few precious seconds.

The sweetest of smiles breaks out on Rohit's face, the equivalent of a hundred hellos.

Or, Rohit extends a hand tentatively.

Or, Rohit says a 'hi' that is just about audible, but sounds like Mozart's *Symphony No. 40* in G Minor K. 550 to the mother.

Or, Rohit looks deep into the Milky Way, but says a loud 'hi'.

Or, Rohit looks straight into Sheena's eyes and says a crisp 'hi'.

Or, Rohit just glances at Sheena—one more way of saying 'hi'.

This simple exchange of greetings is so important for people with autism. To be given the time and the opportunity to:

1. Process that somebody known to them has suddenly come up.
2. Process the identity of that person.
3. Process the greeting that person is making.
4. Process the suggestion made by the mother.
5. Convert the suggestion into an action.

It is not kind to shush a person with autism when he is trying to say or signal something.

It is not kind to pat him on the head and move away.

It is not kind to expect him to respond instantaneously.

It is not kind to bombard him with multiple instructions such as 'Say hi', 'Come on', 'Quickly say hi', *'Chalo, hi bol do'*.

Being kind is when you make an effort to look into Rohit's eyes, greet him and give him a few seconds of quiet time to acknowledge you.

Be that person in Rohit's life who opens gateways of communication with him by gifting him a few seconds of your time and your acceptance.

When Jayashree and Krishna went on a school trip to Mahabaleshwar, CP suggested that we go to Shirdi with Lakshmi and Jayanthi.

The highlight of the trip was a visit to the beautiful new Shirdi Sai Baba Museum. There are four shows in the museum and visitors must follow a very strict protocol. A blue paper band is strapped onto the wrist of every visitor and must be displayed before entering each show.

Suddenly, CP stood before me. He was on the phone, but his face spoke volumes and he gestured towards Lakshmi and waved a torn blue band.

'Oh, my god, CP, how did you tear your band?'

Almost jumping, CP gestured towards Lakshmi again.

'Oh, she tore her band. Why?'

Dirty look.

'I mean, how terrible.'

'Lakshmi, why did you tear your band? Foolish girl!'

Lakshmi smiled and said, 'Say sorry. Say sorry.'

Jayanthi held her hand up to remove her own band.

I shouted, 'No,' and held her arm.

CP got off the phone and we moved towards the queue.

Lakshmi breezed past the security guard who yelled and called her back. She came back obligingly and he looked sternly at her bare wrist.

CP stepped up with an apologetic expression and displayed the torn band.

The guard gave him a speaking look and let them both pass.

CP, fully aware of my state of mirth, avoided looking at me altogether.

The second show was a 5D animation movie. Lakshmi and CP made their Laurel and Hardy presentation again. This time, the guard looked disbelieving, and I am sure he felt CP had torn the band. Not used to seeing an apologetic expression on CP's face, I was having a field day.

We went for the third show. This time CP got ahead of Lakshmi and earnestly explained, 'Er … er … sorry … she has torn the band … See, it is in my pocket.'

The security guard was trying to understand what CP was saying but he was distracted by three things. Just try to imagine the scene from the poor guard's eyes:

1. A grave man incongruously holding a torn band and offering hasty explanations.
2. Two teenage girls, one smiling and trying to edge past her father, and the second obligingly holding out her hand in a fixed pose.
3. An amply built lady with a big bindi and lashings of kajal who looked as if she should be playing the mother-in-law in an Ekta Kapoor serial, shaking with mirth.

I don't remember my marriage vows. In Tamilian weddings, the bride does not have to say anything. Which is a good thing because I have not made any verbal commitment to CP.

Many years later, I reminded him about this feature of our relationship.

He had come home late in the evening. I sat at the dining table with a big vat of green peas that I was shelling while simultaneously advising my children about various real and imagined things.

Enter Urmila didi. '*Mil gaya, mil gaya* (Found it)!' she bleated loudly. I tried to take the object from her subtly but with CP right there, subterfuge became a challenge.

'What is it?' he asked in a deceptively pleasant voice.

'Nothing,' I said brightly, and slunk away.

I never went back to shelling the peas.

I could hear him ask Jayashree, 'What were you looking for?'

'Nothing, Appa. Nothing.'

'Here,' I said helpfully and passed the object to her. Her fingers closed over it and she scuttled away.

CP has been this family's problem-solver from the start, with 2025 being his twenty-first year doing so. He has a robust belief that we do not possess his logical faculties.

He followed me to my room and looked around but could not find any criminal activity.

He came back.

'Lakshmi is shouting, "Fan, fan". Why?' CP said, going into Lakshmi's room.

The fan was rotating but it was at a slow speed.

He turned to twist the regulator and found it missing. There was nothing but a stubby portion protruding out of its former location.

'Can you tell me what you have done with the regulator?'

'See, CP, it's like this. You don't face the issues that I do.'

'Leave all that. Where is the regulator?'

'That's what I am telling you about. Lakshmi runs the fan at full speed even with the AC on. The room becomes too cold. So I tried counselling Lakshmi, then I tried switching off the AC. I hid the AC remote. She found it. So I set the fan at a medium level and yanked the regulator out.'

'Yanked? What's that?'

CP always says, 'Stick to simple English. I studied at Vani Vidyalaya.'

'Pulled,' I explained helpfully.

'You pulled the entire regulator out?'

'What entire? It is so small! Wait, I will show it to you. Jayashree, Jayashree!' I shouted gratefully, trying to garner my forces.

Jayashree came out and passed something from her palm to mine.

I opened my palm and there lay a regulator in its pristine glory.

CP prised it away from me and asked, 'Why are you passing it around like Sai Baba vibhuthi?'

At this point Jayashree continued the Amar Chitra Katha narrative.

'Appa,' she chimed. 'See, once Lakshmi came to know that regulators can be dismantled, she did it across the house.'

CP marched to the living room switch area and saw the remains of the Harappan dynasty.

He stood in silence while I supplied the voiceover.

'Lakshmi has hidden them somewhere. We can't find them. Only one is there. We are preserving it carefully.'

'You mean to say that you are using one regulator across five rooms and the living room?'

'See, I've figured out a formula. There are ten fans in the house including Sai Baba's fan. Lakshmi has not touched Baba's fan. Out of the nine remaining fans, at least six are in use most of the time. So we keep the regulator in the room where it was last used and as and when we need to adjust the speed of the fan in another room, we borrow the regulator.'

CP took the regulator and tried fixing it back. As soon as he removed his hand, the regulator fell off. He picked it up, reinstated it and pushed it in aggressively. It plopped down.

I quickly picked it up.

CP tenderly escorted Jayashree away from me and went to his room and lay down.

I could hear his sigh of relief as he settled on his cane chair. I could hear the rustle of the *Economic Times*. I could hear the voices of Sun TV and then the sound I had been awaiting: the click of the fan switch.

There was an ominous silence.

'Here,' I said helpfully. 'You keep the regulator for some time.'

He regrettably did not show any gratitude at my largesse as he took it and twisted it in.

Then it plopped off.

See, that's why I said I did not chant any marriage vows. Only the priest who bound us in holy matrimony went on and on. However, none of the sacred verses refer to any commitment on my part that I will not touch or disfigure or dismantle or cause any harm to the fan regulators in my house.

There is something about tea that brings people together.

CP wandered out of his den into the kitchen. It was nearly 10 p.m. Since the kitchen has been patented in my name since 11

September 2002 (the date of our holy matrimony), I immediately enquired, 'What do you want?'

'Tea,' he said briefly.

I shouted out, 'There is only one small piece of ginger left in the fridge. I am saving it for tomorrow's tea.'

He started complaining vigorously while Krishna called out, 'Give me tea also.'

CP added some water to the vessel.

Jayashree peeked out. 'What are you people doing?'

CP was resigned. 'Do you want tea?' he asked, and added more water.

By this time, the small piece of ginger was overwhelmed in the vessel of ever deeper water.

I said, 'Jayanthi loves tea with biscuits. You can't leave out Tomato either.'

CP took out a bigger vessel.

He noticed me peering out of the kitchen window. By this time, he had the healthy suspicion that his cup of tea was not going according to plan.

'What are you looking at?'

'I am just checking whether Madhuri-ji's kitchen light is on,' I said.

'Why?'

'When we want to borrow something from each other's kitchen at night, we check if the other person's kitchen light is on. That means they are awake,' I explained.

Not impressed at all, he said, 'Stop borrowing for the kitchen. If you don't have something, do without it.'

I countered, 'You are talking as if I am going from house to house. Madhuri-ji and I depend on each other for kitchen emergencies.'

I came back after two minutes, triumphantly holding aloft a huge piece of ginger. I said brightly, 'At least twenty rupees' worth of ginger free.'

I freely admit that I did not deserve a response.

The cauldron of tea boiled merrily with a generous quantity of pounded ginger. Just as CP started to spoon in the tea powder, I halted him yet again.

I took out my tea mug, squeezed half a lime into it and poured half a cup of boiling ginger water into the strainer with the tea powder. A beautiful golden tea emerged. I reached for the sugar, saw an ominous aura gather around CP, and hastily picked up the Sugar Free sachet instead.

Finally, tea powder and milk were added, the water boiled, and five cups of tea were poured out.

I watched enviously as sugar was added to the kids' tea. CP was born boringly virtuous and he stuck to Sugar Free.

Finally, when we congregated around the dining table with our respective mugs and slowly sipped our tea, an atmosphere of bonhomie and acceptance descended. It had all started with one cup of tea and created so much work and confusion. Still, this tea is more flavourful because it is being consumed by the people who matter.

Nothing like tea to iron out the irritating wrinkles of life.

We were out shopping—Krishna, Lakshmi, Jayanthi, Jayashree and I.

When we were finally about to exit, the guard stopped me and, pointing to Lakshmi, said in Hindi: 'Madam, what is wrong with her?'

'She has autism.'

Pointing to Jayanthi and Jayashree, she said, 'What about them?'

'Jayanthi also has autism.'

'How do you look after them?'

Before I could answer, she continued, 'What about the future? Who will take care of them?'

'There are many people like Lakshmi and Jayanthi. Their way of communicating and working is different. They need some extra support.'

She pointed to Krishna. 'He also has some problem?'

Krishna was impervious and continued talking to another security guard to learn where the parking area was located. He took me by the arm, gave a small shove to Lakshmi, who was checking out the sanitiser spray, and we moved out and on.

I can't deny feeling sad as I got into the car and we drove away.

The fact is, Lakshmi and Jayanthi don't look 'normal' anymore because they are not protected by the anonymity that infancy provides.

What is normal?

Dress code: I let them choose what they are comfortable in, as long as their clothes are neat and they are reasonably covered. If they choose to attend a wedding in a t-shirt and track pants, so be it.

Repetitive movements: Jayanthi hums, Lakshmi taps on things that interest her.

Eye contact: Lakshmi can ignore you so completely that you begin to wonder if you exist.

Body posture: Totally unselfconscious, whether we are sitting in a chair at home or are in an office or a shop.

Do they need a chaperone in public spaces? Most certainly, yes!

Do they know how to cross the road? No.

Can they navigate an airport or a mall, or go to a shop and buy a loaf of bread without assistance? No.

Do they look and behave 'normal'? No.

Their vulnerability, their behaviour issues, their special kind of communication, their sense of dressing and body language sets them apart.

As the lady asked, what will happen later?

The security guard was genuinely distraught, like many others when they come face to face with a disability.

But Lakshmi and Jayanthi are also forms of life on earth. Just as a duckling or a chicken or any creature hatches from an egg, sways drunkenly on fragile legs, and spends every day of its existence fighting for survival, people with disabilities are fighters.

They are warriors, meant to teach the world what it is to be unequal, to be vulnerable, and yet to not give up and survive.

I told the security guard, 'Just as you are being considerate to Lakshmi and Jayanthi, there are people who support them and understand them.'

She smiled and nodded.

Jayashree came back home two days ago, cheeks flushed with irritation.

'What happened?'

'So irritating, Amma! Krishna and I had gone to Pooja Stores to buy bread.'

'Okay.'

'We paid and were waiting for the change. The shopkeeper looked at us meditatively and said, '*Tum dono thode chhote dikhte ho. Complan vomplan nahi peete ho kya* (You two look small for your age. Don't you drink something like Complan)?'

'What? Oh my god!'

I laughed and laughed and laughed.

'He really said that?'

'Ya. I dragged Krishna out of the shop quickly because you never know ... though Krishna is always cool, he can lose his temper.'

'Did Krishna say anything?'

'No, but the way he stared at the shopkeeper. I dragged him out.'

'Thank god I was not there with you. He would have said, '*Tum thode mote ho. Herbalife verbalife nahi peete ho kya* (You look fat. Don't you take things like Herbalife)?'

1. Yes, we are more grown up, though our height remains way below average.
2. Our hearts know the song of acceptance. We care for each other, watch out for each other, lend a helping hand when we can, know how to be respectful to others.
3. We've entered college and have developed an active conscience that guides us to handle our newfound freedom.
4. We love our food. We love to talk. We dress simply. We have big dreams.
5. When we look in the mirror, we see short people with strong hearts, active minds and sound conscience, and with a long way to go.

All the health drinks in the world could not have made us grow the way we have.

There has never been a disability on either side of our family. The autism diagnoses left us in shock, with a lingering sadness and the sense of all our dreams being washed away.

Prayer helped, but the prayer was not peaceful.

It was a fury, a rampage.

I recall that for an entire Margazhi season, I woke up at two in the morning, showered in cold water, wore wet clothes and chanted, 'Hare Rama, Hare Rama, Rama, Rama, Hare, Hare, Hare Krishna, Hare Krishna, Krishna, Krishna, Hare, Hare'.

It is said that when this shloka is chanted a hundred and eight times, the lord appears before you.

I think the universe had enough of me and decided to teach me that some things in life can't be cured like a lock being untwisted by a key.

Some things in life are just meant to be, like autism.

Some things must be respected and empowered, like autism.

That year, I became a Sai devotee and stopped going out like a fisherman every morning to try and capture god in my net.

I still wake up early in the morning during Margazhi. I have aged and can't think of showering in cold water. I ensure that I put on the geyser for some time the night before. Wet clothes are out of the question. I wear comfortable clothes and drape an old dupatta around myself to keep warm. The lord has become a cherished friend to whom I lift my eyes in trust.

On Vaikuntha Ekadasi, many devotees go to the temple early in the morning. Many devotees fast. Some stay awake the whole night and chant his name.

Some, like Lakshmi, casually talk to him and share a biscuit packet with him. Some time ago, I saw Lakshmi munching on Hide and Seek biscuits at the dining table. I realised with horror that she had gone up to Sai Baba's altar and taken them from his plate. I ticked her off roundly. Weeks passed. One day, I caught Lakshmi picking up the biscuit packet from Sai Baba's plate and actually asking him, 'Take, take?' before taking it.

What could be a more enriching relationship than this where Lakshmi believes he is there and talks to him so casually and freely?

That day, I envied her and set her free.

We've been invited to attend a wedding today. When we are invited out, we first have to locate clothes that fit the 'smart casuals' tag. Some time ago, one of our volunteers (the Chakrapani family does not have friends, it has volunteers) had taken the children shopping for shoes and bought the girls sandals. I fished them out.

CP, not to be outdone, produced earrings. He put tiny, comfortable earrings in both their ears and looked at me victoriously.

I am an autism mom. Over the years, acceptance has established itself in me as soundly as the extra kilos that I carry in my body. I smiled appreciatively and waited, while cutting ginger for the

Sunday special lunch that I have been feeding the family free of cost since September 2002.

Within seven minutes, Lakshmi casually touched her earrings while rocking in the rocking chair. CP roared, 'You remove them and watch out!'

'That's all very well, CP. When she takes a nap in the afternoon, that's when she will remove them and we will be frantically searching under the pillows, blankets, etc.'

CP paled visibly because we spend precious hours searching for our belongings on a daily basis already.

Grumbling, he removed her earrings. Lakshmi continued rocking peaceably.

CP turned and found Jayanthi looking at him meaningfully. He pretended not to understand and went to pick up his cup of tea. She followed him. He went into his room and opened the cupboard to put away Lakshmi's earrings. She followed him and tentatively touched her ears.

I cut away at the ginger, trying not to let my mirth show.

She emerged without her earrings and CP followed, looking at me suspiciously.

I burst out laughing.

'Let's put them on in the evening. They will be happy to wear them, CP, but not at home.'

Home is not only where the heart is. Home is comfort. Home is ragged chappals. Home is frayed clothes. Home is chucking away adornments and being free.

———⊷⊙⊛⊙⊶———

I have been looking for a helper for daily cleaning at my home. A lady walked in yesterday, accompanied by another person. As we started speaking with each other, she asked me, 'Does Lakshmi live here?'

'Lakshmi?' I could not believe that she knew my Lakshmi.

'This is Lakshmi's home?'

'Yes! How do you know?'

A very odd smile broke out on her face.

'Have you ever met Lakshmi?'

'She is the one who goes to that place where certain kind of people go.'

It was not a nice smile. It was not a smile of humour. It was something else. A strange mix of a jeer and contempt.

My breath caught in my throat, but nevertheless I chatted with her calmly.

I work with a fantastic bunch of youngsters with autism and other disabilities. Nevertheless, this smile was an arrow that successfully pierced my skin.

What had Lakshmi done? Had she talked to herself while walking to the centre? Had she tried to approach an unknown person? Had her autism become apparent through her body language or gaze? What had happened?

Autism is not a part-time problem. It pervades like water and nutrients in soil and like oxygen in the air. It cannot be separated from the human. Sometimes an odd gaze, a dreamy smile, a cacophony of giggles, a sudden outburst of affection for someone, a conversation with nobody in particular—it can take any form.

I invited the same lady to visit the centre. I wanted to show her around and let her take a piece of the purity and 'being oneself' that people with autism possess.

However, as a mother and like countless other mothers, I face these needles on and off. There is no Soframycin ointment for these wounds. Like animals in the forest that heal after the most grievous wounds and walk the jungle again, these mothers remove the arrows and continue walking.

Have you ever played Snakes and Ladders? Felt the relief of getting a ladder and the shock of a snake that suddenly drags you down?

I have been playing Snakes and Ladders for sixteen years now. Like millions of mothers of children with autism all over the world, I climb ladders every day. We climb the ladder of assessment. We reach the snake of diagnosis and plummet downwards. Wiping away our tears resolutely, we climb the ladder of therapy and intervention. We reach the snake of the therapist who will solve all our problems in our lives, but is missing. We trudge up the ladder of academics. We reach the snake of the academic plateau. We once again find the ladder of future opportunities. We reach the snake of behaviours that make our children their own enemies. Never mind. We climb the ladder of behaviour modification.

In the meantime, we have an ever-present snake of running expenses and managing money and securing the future for all the family members. We clutch the hands of our spouses/partners/parents as we continue looking for one more ladder.

As our children become slightly older, we see a big fat snake that reminds us—what will happen after us?

We climb the ladder of lifetime care. We see snakes everywhere, reminding us to work harder, to teach our children to embrace adulthood, and to try our best to secure their future from every possible angle.

We gasp and gasp and search for a ladder. We keep searching for a ladder.

At these times, if there is no ladder in sight, we must go into the world and search for bricks, for stones, for ropes, for steel, for any material that is as sturdy as Mother Earth, that is as resilient as the sky, the sun, the moon and the stars that appear in our lives every day.

We will make that ladder, my friends. We will climb that ladder, my friends. We will climb it with our children and emerge into a space in which we will pour all our energy, our values, our honesty, our love for every child, and we will fashion a world for our children. A world that we will lovingly leave behind for them so they can continue living with responsible people who they care for and who care for them.

Sometimes we don't want our children to grow up. Sometimes, unfortunately, they don't grow up and parenting stands frozen in time.

Jayanthi took ten years to learn to have a bath on her own—from year five to fifteen—and three years to manage her period. Lakshmi took two years for the bath and six months for her period.

During these years, I could not stop living as a mother or as a woman. I managed my household, cooked food, met friends, attended family functions. I smiled. I looked sorted.

Then I would come back home and go back through a grim, mind-numbing routine.

1. Teach Jayanthi to change inside the bathroom—a space that ideally nobody should share with you.
2. Teach her to identify her period and tell someone about it.
3. Teach the use of a period bag that protects her privacy.
4. Teach the 'turn around and check' test—have I left the bathroom clean?
5. Switch from being a mother inside the bathroom to being a mother outside the bathroom, so all I need to do is verbally give reminders and she cleans up herself.

There are days we can't go out, there are weddings we can't attend, or meetings we can't take because they fall on 'THOSE' days.

What does an autism parent do when a daughter has her period, when a son has discovered the joys of masturbation and does it anywhere, anytime—after all it's his body. When the parent has to painstakingly teach the son to take the option of a closed door when soothing his cravings.

There are places we can't go, like theatres, where the self-talking or humming, which the person with autism uses as a mechanism to calm himself down, will most definitely not be appreciated by the others in the audience.

So, is the mother to watch the movie and enjoy her popcorn? Or reassure her son, be conscious of his every breath, ask him if he wants to go to the washroom, try to call a dignified halt to eating snacks nonstop in a public space, try to stop herself from wiping the mouth of her twenty-five-year-old son in public and urge him, with a napkin, to, 'Wipe your mouth, wipe'?

It goes on and on and on as we see our friends sending their children out for sleepovers, sending them away for higher studies, letting them migrate for a new job and laughingly complain, 'I just don't see Arjun anymore', while longing for that mysterious and elusive happiness for ourselves and our children.

At such times, you square your shoulders, pick up the phone, and talk to a fellow parent who will help you find your peace.

OR

You pick up the phone and talk to your parents, whose baby *you* are.

The grandparents whose grief has never gone away. The grandparent who has missed out on long conversations with a beloved grandchild, who knows that he will not get to give a cheque for higher studies or plan a monstrously expensive wedding gift.

The grandparents who have finally stopped dreaming of a miracle cure and resolutely started planning the future of the grandchild.

The grandparent who will pick up the phone every time you call, and in a voice quivering with age but resolute with strength, say, 'You can do it, you will do it.'

And we will go on.

Autism parenting. Pick up the phone and talk.

There are few things in a home that generate as much comfort as a bowl of Maggi.

Over the past few years, the children have been making their own Maggi on Saturday nights, which are the resident cook's—namely, me—evening off.

A huge vat of water is kept to boil on the stove.

Out comes the bright yellow packet that makes a sigh of collective joy go up and the heart go pitter pat. Plus Nestle has helpfully introduced industrial sized packs meant for families like ours that buy Maggi by weight: '*Bhaiya zara char kilo Maggi dena* (Can you give us four kilos of Maggi, please)?'

Chopped veggies go in, some green chillies, then the Maggi, the masala, a teaspoon of salt and a big dash of chilli powder.

As the fragrance of Maggi emanates enticingly, the only person who remains totally impervious is our resident Iron Man, CP. He wanders into the crowded kitchen and casts a glance at his children, who are doing different things as the Maggi is being prepared.

Jayashree actively makes the Maggi.

Lakshmi takes out four plates and one katori and lays them out neatly.

Jayanthi looks anxious.

Jayashree finally lowers the Maggi vat.

Lakshmi, who watches with undisguised impatience, adds a spoon of Amul butter, giving the Maggi a heavenly glow, the kind of glow that is found in Amar Chitra Kathas when describing the court of Lord Indra, etc.

Jayanthi inches forward like a puppy and looks even more anxious.

Krishna finally makes his appearance, compelled by the intoxicating fragrance of Maggi.

Iron Man assembles his plate of roti sabzi and gratefully escapes the kitchen.

Jayashree leaves one small katori of Maggi aside for Lakshmi, who sees a second helping as her rightful due, before proceeding to divide the rest of the Maggi into four equal parts.

During my pregnancy, the sonography reports would list the weight of each baby, helpfully numbered as Quadruplet 1, Quadruplet 2 and so on. The stark differences in the weight of the babies would cause me great anxiety.

'Why is it that only Q3 is growing properly, doctor?'

'Mrs Chakrapani, Quad 3 is the Bhima among your four who is eating their share!'

Today, Q3 Lakshmi continues ruling the roost with a katori for that wee bit extra!

Jayanthi does not drink cold water. The other day, she was in the kitchen and Krishna passed her a glass of water. I watched as he added some cold water to the glass from the fridge.

'Chumploo (one of Jayanthi's many pet names) does not drink cold water,' I told Krishna.

'I know, Amma. But she should try everything. If there's only cold water available, she should be able to drink it, isn't it?'

I always marvel at the network of people who try to empower, protect and secure Jayanthi. Lakshmi treats Jayanthi like a pet puppy without a leash. Jayashree and Jayanthi have a matching gentleness and bond like dewdrops on roses, seamlessly. Krishna drapes a blanket over her when she goes to sleep, gives her the iPad when she looks lost, patiently plays catch ball with her, and rags her boisterously, making Jayanthi's eyes widen with alarm.

Anil, our driver, says, '*Bhabhi, Jayanthi insaan nahin, gai hai. Itni bholi, haath pakdo toh chali aati hai* (Jayanthi is not human. She is a calf who will follow anyone trustingly).'

Every morning, Anil escorts the girls to the Together Foundation centre. He wanders into the house and waters the plants on the terrace while we shout in unison, 'Jayanthi, go to the bathroom. Jayanthi, put on your shoes.'

By the time she is done, Anil is back and he extends his hand to Jayanthi. I choke with tears as I see her clutching his hand and peaceably walking with him.

People with autism are capable, yet vulnerable. They communicate but with multiple and varied roadblocks. They constantly work towards independence, but need strong, responsible, incorruptible people to help them negotiate the pathways of life.

There is so much that we as a family learn from Jayanthi. It is no less than sitting in a forest and renewing ourselves with energy.

Jayanthi, she who was christened Squirrel by the nurses at Bombay Hospital. Every time one called her, she would burrow into the pillow, hiding her face with shyness.

I placed my takeaway bag of fries at the McDonald's counter and asked for another bag of fries. It was inordinately delayed and the staff apologised, disposed of the existing takeaway, and gave me two bags of fresh fries. It was all done so fast, I gaped.

'Why did you throw that out and waste it?'

'No, ma'am, the fries had got cold, so I gave you fresh product.'

The staff are so confident, well-trained and know what to do. I sighed with envy!

At the end of the day, I am an autism professional and not a businesswoman. That's someone else's job that I have been trying to do for ten years.

In what now seems like another life, I had worked in advertising, at Lintas, Rediffusion and Clarion Advertising Services. The experience had drilled in me an emphasis on detailing and the search for perfect presentation. All these learnings came to the fore when I founded Together Foundation in 2015 and started operating a bakery. I worked tirelessly with my team of teachers and adults to develop an FSSAI-certified bakery with products, pricing and packaging that stood out with their elegance and simplicity.

At every stage, I used to think of Mayuri Vir, who I had the good fortune of working with at Clarion. She made me rewrite a letter to a client seventeen times and finally gave it such an impeccable finishing touch that, long after this incident in 1997, I can still remember standing in her cabin, looking over her shoulder and wishing I had written that letter.

After so much effort over ten years, has Together succeeded?

Yes and no.

Yes, because, one, we deliver industry-standard products to customers all over Mumbai, and two, we serve people with autism and empower them with work skills in a respectful and highly motivated environment. We are funded and deliver affordable and accessible services to people with autism all over Mumbai and the country.

But the fact remains that we have not yet cracked a sound business model. As a non-profit organisation, our expenses in serving the disability sector are high. We don't earn much and even the stipends we pay come from funding. We can't deliver high volume orders. We need time.

If there is one area where Together Foundation stands shoulder to shoulder with McDonald's and even an inch ahead, it is brand experience. What's that? It is when a customer picks up a Together product and knows that this high-quality product comes from an extraordinary place and reads the story of our extraordinary cause: a story that Kiran Khalap wrote for us and that inspires me to continue trying to be a businesswoman.

To have the guts to imagine meeting the CEO of McDonald's.

'Hello, Mr Kempczinski! I run a business too!'

Krishna went to college for the first time after lockdown. I fell on him like an overweight Labrador the moment he returned home. He bore my onslaught with equanimity as I followed him, asking questions.

'Krishna! How was college?'
'Good, Amma!'
'What happened?'
'Nothing.'
'How many people turned up?'
'Around twenty-five.'
'Any friends?'
'All my friends came.'
'How was your first meeting with them?'
'Good, Amma. Cool.'
'Did they rag you?'
'Why would they rag me? Of course, they didn't.'
'I was worried they would comment on your height.'
'No, Amma. But Ajay tried his best!'
'Ajay Sir! Why? How did he enter the picture?'
'I met him downstairs when I came back from college. He was working out.'
'Okay! So? What did he say?'
'He said, "*Sab ladke itne lambe rahe honge. Aap toh itne chote ho* (The other boys must have been much taller than you! You would have looked so short next to them)."'
I gasped. 'Are you serious?'
'Ya.'
'So what did you say?'
'Nothing.'
'You did not reply at all?'
'I just said, "Ya, ya", and got into the lift.'
'Krishna, that was totally uncalled for!'
'Amma, chill. Why would I worry about what he thinks of me?'
Jayashree chimed in. 'If someone had said this to me, I would have talked about it forever, given that guy a piece of my mind, and not forgotten it till the day I died. After dying, I would come back as a bhooth and haunt him till he said, "Sorry. Forgive me. I will never comment on your height or pass comments at anyone again in this life and other lives."'

I nodded vigorously. 'Absolutely!'

When do you realise that your son has grown up? Not when he starts earning. Not when he gets qualified for a job. Not even when he shoots up in height.

After this display of tolerance towards others and sense of self-worth, I felt the next generation of this family was ready to take its place in the world.

Krishna, he who was nicknamed Elephant (Yanai papa in Tamil) by the nurses at Bombay Hospital.

In the twenty years that I've been in Mumbai, I've successfully learnt two phrases in Marathi.

One is 'radu nako', which translates to 'don't cry'.

On Lakshmi's first night out of the NICU after she had been handed to me, she was on twenty-five millilitres of NAN (powdered milk) every two hours.

I faithfully gave it to her on time, but she kept bawling and the ayahs would chant, 'Radu nako, radu nako.'

The head of NICU visited us the next morning and I looked at her with bloodshot eyes. 'Give her more NAN, Sangeetha, she is hungry.'

Simple.

The second phrase in Marathi is beautiful: three words with which you can absolve yourself of every vestige of responsibility. This is something my house helps have taught me. They say it every time something is broken or something goes missing.

The trick is to say the three words very casually. You should not stop doing whatever you are doing. Continue with your work and casually say the words. There is no rebuttal or comeback invented for these three words. They are all-powerful and cloak you in permanent protection.

I have started using these words as a self-insurance policy in my home because the Chakrapani family is always searching for something. Unfortunately, these three words translated into English do not carry the same effect. They pale in comparison to the thunderous utterance in Marathi. But CP will smell a hundred rats if I try the Marathi version, so I say the watered-down version in English: 'I don't know.'

The Marathi stunner is '*Mala mayith nai.*'

Super!

So, to add some thunder, I emphasise 'Iiiiiiii don't know,' and continue reading/cooking/writing with a feverish expression on my face.

CP has not been fooled, of course. The man was born with the hat and magnifying glass that Conan Doyle gave Holmes. So the weak English version has not worked its magic.

The Marathi original awaits its turn.

Mala mayith nai.

Casually.

I love it.

Conversations with Jayashree

Conversation 1

'Jayashree, is that your new phone?'

'Yes.'

'Then keep it carefully. Whatever you did with your old phone, don't do with your new phone.'

'Amma, this is not a new phone. Appa does not believe in buying new phones.'

'It's not a new phone?'

'For me, it is a new phone because I am using it for the first time. But the phone is not new. This is your old ka old phone.'

'Old ka old?'
'Yes. You had an old phone?'
'Yes, I had.'
'Then Appa took your old phone and gave you a new phone when you threatened to take out a morcha holding a banner?'
'Yes.'
'By the way, that new phone he gave you was also not a new phone.'
'Oh!'
'But the old phone that he took away from you had another ancestor, your previous old phone.'
'Okay.'
'That old ka old phone he had repaired and gave it to me.'
'Oh.'
'It is so old that we don't recognise it and feel it is new.'

Conversation 2

'Amma, do you realise that you are not okay?'
'What do you mean?'
'You don't read books these days. You don't watch TV at all. When did you last watch a movie? Come, sit with me. Close your laptop. Put your phone down. I have identified at least five movies for you. No violence. Happy endings. LKG-level romance.'

Conversation 3

'Somebody has kidnapped my pants. Amma, you know I like my old clothes.'
'Jayashree, those pants are not old. They are torn.'
'But, Amma, they are old and that's why they are torn. We should value them. I've made a senior citizens' section in my cupboard. Give me back the pants. I will put them there.'

Jayashree, she who was nicknamed Butterfly by the NICU nurses at Bombay Hospital.

Our morning helper is making khana for us today. I sang a ditty from a Rajinikanth movie, indicating my mood.

'*Aaj Sunday hai, aaj Sunday hai, toh din me daaru peene ka din hai* (Today is Sunday, we drink all day)!'

CP asked me with great civility about what the helper was willing to make and therefore what veggies he had to buy. Our fridge is not working so we have to buy fresh edibles on a daily basis. He got ready to go out.

'I will come with you,' Jayshree said.

CP looked gratified at the show of support.

Jayanthi looked at Jayashree.

'Okay, you also come,' said CP.

There was a resigned note in his tone of voice because two things would immediately follow.

'Jayanthi, go to the bathroom' x four times.

'Jayanthi, put on your shoes' x six times.

Lakshmi rushed forward anxiously because Jayanthi is the Barbie doll that the universe gifted her on 19 January 2004.

So Lakshmi was invited to put on her shoes.

Krishna knew what was expected of him as CP looked a wee bit anxious at the sight of the group he had to escort to the sabzi mandi in the environs of Poonam Nagar.

There is no doubt that both CP and I have aged because we have escorted the brood on shopping excursions for years, starting from when they were just four years old. By now, managing the brood is a breeze. However, we find ourselves talking more and more about keeping ourselves strong, motivated and charged with enthusiasm for the road that lies ahead. We will be like Tom Sawyer, who converted his chore of painting the fence of his house into an envied activity. People will look at us and exclaim, 'I wish I had quadruplets! What fun they are having!'

A few weeks ago, Jayanthi went up to Jayashree and pointed to her ear. Mystified, Jayashree made her sit down and looked in.

Nothing.

'Amma, Jayanthi is showing her ear again and again but there is nothing there. No problem.'

I made an appointment with the ENT who, thank heavens, had the patience to allow Jayanthi to talk to him.

'Jayanthi, this is Doctor. Doctor, this is Jayanthi. She has autism and uses sign language. Jayanthi, tell Doctor what happened.'

Doctor is kind enough to wait that precious five seconds for Jayanthi to process my request in a new environment with a new person. Then she lifts her hand to her ear, pulls it and leans towards the doctor.

Praise god! She successfully asked a third party for help.

Later that night, I was deeply asleep and woke up to a murmur and a gentle tap on my shoulder. Startled, I turned and switched on the light.

It was Jayanthi. She had got out of bed at night, walked in the dark and come in search of me to say goodnight.

I hugged her.

'Goodnight, Jayanthi.'

'Goodnight.'

'Goodnight.'

'Sairam.'

I could have gone on forever.

Finally, she got up from my bed where she was sitting.

My instinctive response was to escort Jayanthi to her room and see her get into bed.

It was a growing-up moment for both of us when she turned, looked at me peaceably and went back to her room to sleep.

I switched off the light and went to sleep, awash with gratitude to the universe for helping this mother and daughter take a step forward.

Keyes High School in Hyderabad, my first school, had a shloka as the school prayer. I developed a love for singing hymns at St. Mary's School, Poona. Mother Nature was the primary deity at Sharada Mandir School, Goa, with not even a compound wall separating us from the glory of Miramar Beach.

We grew up happily and never felt our individual faiths were compromised by singing loudly the sonorous and time-honoured tracks of another faith.

Recently, I visited the Cloistered Carmel Convent near my home to hand over clothes for the needy. It was seven in the evening. There was no bell, only a door knocker. The door opened and a nun stood there looking at me silently. I hastily explained my reason for coming over. She motioned with one hand—wait—and disappeared for a few minutes.

I could not see anyone or hear anything. Then I heard the rhythmic sound of words: a faint murmur that resonated within the silent walls of the convent.

The nun came back.

'Sister, what sound is that?'

'Prayer,' she said briefly.

I handed over the clothes and found myself unable to leave.

Sister waited silently as I struggled to find words.

Finally, I said, 'May I pray for some time before leaving?'

She motioned me towards the chapel.

I entered and looked to my right, where I could see the Cross.

Then she spoke. 'Here is the body of Christ.'

I jerked my head to the left and saw a long table with a shroud on it.

Such was her faith and conviction, such was the intensity of devotion in her voice, her carriage, in every fibre of her being, that I could barely breathe.

I sat quietly for a few minutes.

She escorted me out. 'I will pray for you,' she said, and the door closed.

I saw this kind of indomitable faith in the maulvis when I took all four children, then aged just one, to the masjid in the early hours of the morning.

I stood there with the ayah, each of us holding two babies. As elderly men came out of early morning namaz and moved towards my babies, tears coursed down my cheeks. They blessed the babies and moved away.

How many mothers have stood in front of them? How many hopes, how much desperation have these men seen and encountered?

My children and I have different ways of praying.

We were at a temple in Coonoor where one of the deities is sought after by students writing exams.

I called the children over excitedly.

'Pray here.'

Krishna stood there. Not content with his silence, I said, 'You must pray, Krishna.'

He replied, 'Amma, if we work hard, we will do well.'

I felt so ashamed.

What was I doing to my children? Here they are visiting temples with open and uncomplicated minds, and here I am trying to introduce the concept of compulsorily praying *for* something, to ask for something.

If we lived in Chennai or any other part of South India, the atmosphere on Diwali would be reverberating with the sights and sounds and smells of the Tamilian community in celebration.

Even in Mumbai, we Tamilians wake up at about 3.30 in the morning, when the lady of the house applies warmed til oil on everyone's head. Then everyone has a bath, wears new clothes, and prostrates in the puja room and before elders.

Then we start calling up family members before 5 a.m. to shout, 'Happy Diwali. *Ganga snanam acha*?' (The river Ganga is supposed to be present in all water in the wee hours of the morning.) And if the others still haven't got their act together, one feels very virtuous and victorious. Then we burst crackers at that time of the morning before having breakfast, in which idli and sweets are a must.

In the South, there is a great sense of camaraderie. Here, CP and I feel foolish, which is actually a proprietary value used and marketed by the Chakrapani family ever since the quadruplets were born.

So, to overcome the feeling of foolishness, we start building the hype a few days before Diwali.

'Wow, it's Diwali!'

'What fun!'

'We will wake up EARLY in the morning.'

'Great, ya!'

'We will put M.S. Subbulakshmi on full volume in the hall and Sun TV on full volume in one more room for a special effect.'

'Great, ya!'

'Ya, we will apply oil, bathe and wear LOVELY new clothes!'

'Great, ya!'

'Ya, it will be so much fun!'

'Ya, ya!'

'We have to call Bangalore and Chennai and wish them before they call us, so that they know we are also doing what everyone is doing there.'

'Ya, ya, I will call, don't worry.'

'Then we will burst crackers on our terrace, because if we go down and burst them at that time, whatever little respect is left for us in the building will be eroded completely.'

'Great, ya!'

'Then I will slave and make breakfast while you go around and grab the gold earrings from the girls' ears before Lakshmi removes and distributes them among our security guards and before that, take LOTS of photographs to put on the family WhatsApp group so everybody knows that we also know how to wear nice clothes.'

'Great, ya!'
Happy Diwali, Mumbai style, Chakrapani style!

Some years ago, we went on a holiday to Himachal Pradesh. The best part of it was the toy train we boarded from Kalka to Shimla.

CP and I were in a heightened state of excitement. We competed with each other to tell the children about the fun of travelling in a toy train. The natural beauty one could see. That in our own separate childhoods we had never been on a toy train, and now we were actually going to board a TOY train! Imagine, a TOY TRAIN!

The kids were unfailingly polite but I could see their rapidly increasing boredom and wariness as our own excitement increased.

On the morning of the journey, CP and I were briskly ready. We wore our best clothes, those befitting a TOY train. We almost composed an anthem on the joys, novelty, rarity, beauty, specialty, ingenuity, jocundity, velocity, credibility, sentimentality, opportunity, singularity, personality and capacity of the TOY train.

Lakshmi regularly bleated, 'Train, train', so we felt we had managed to make a deep impression on her.

Jayanthi looked as excited as a Zen master on his first ride in a toy train.

Jayashree and Krishna looked manful and excited by turns, as if they had discussed it between themselves. 'First part of the morning you look excited and I will do my thing, second part I will take over and you do your own thing.'

Much before the train started, we ensured window seats for all of us. CP and I had our noses plastered to our windows. The kids were concerned.

'Er ... Amma, Appa ... Right now, we are at the station. Let the train start.'

'Ya, ya, but the moment it starts, start looking outside.'

As the train chugged out, CP and I let out small shrieks of excitement. We left our seats and rushed to the kids' side.

'See, see, the train is moving!'
'Look outside!'
'So beautiful!'
'Wow!'
'So green!'
'See the flowers!'
'What flowers, Amma? Wait till the train moves out of the station.'
'Some more photos.'

There is no doubt that the toy train was an indescribably beautiful experience. All of us fell silent as the train, built in 1898, chugged past small hamlets, hillsides, mountainsides, offering us a panorama of the simple, rich and plentiful beauty of Mother Nature.

I was entranced when the train stopped for a minute or two at a tiny station called Barog. CP had a resigned expression on his face.

'Why are you looking like that?'
'I know what you are going to say.'
'What?'
'CP, let's buy a house and settle down here. We will somehow manage the children here. You will somehow work for HDFC Bank from here.'

'Wow, CP, how did you know? We can't leave this and go back.'
'We have to, Sangeetha. Every time we need this badly, we will make time and come back.'

It's been eight years now and the TOY train beckons again.

We went for a holiday to Dharamshala. Those days, I fretted over my kids and did not enjoy them. Today, I wish I was thirty-five years old again.

If Lakshmi kicked off her shoes in a restaurant, I would calmly put them away and give them back to her after leaving. So what if she ate barefoot?

If Jayanthi did not want to eat dal, I would give her curd, and live and let live.

If Lakshmi squeezed out the toothpaste from the tube, I would keep the paste in a container with a lid and use it up.

If Jayanthi insisted on wearing the same sweater every day, I would let her, and put it out in the sun to air when she slept in the afternoon. So what if the sweater was stained?

We were on a holiday.

I wish I could cuddle them again. I wish I could reassure Jayashree and Krishna again that Lakshmi and Jayanthi are fine. I wish I could have reassured myself then that it's okay to be different.

This wisdom dawns slowly but surely in all parents in the autism family.

But it's not too late.

I have thrown away the clock of twenty-four-hour anxiety. I have thrown away the clock that ticks away and tells me that my children are growing older. Yes, they are growing older. We will learn as we go along. I have thrown away the consciousness of my children having to look picture perfect. So what if their hair is mussed, so what if they are wearing well-worn home clothes that hug them in the warmth of comfort.

Are they safe? Are they happy? Are they kind? Are they learning? Are they active, whether it is shelling peas or baking cookies or folding clothes?

Be happy. Create happy. Stay happy.

Smile.

I have always loved the colour of chocolate and was tempted by an advertisement for hair colour that had Aishwariya Rai showing off her glossy brown locks of hair.

I walked into a very smart-looking beauty salon.

The lady at the front desk was brave and did not bat an eyelid as she took me in with the all-seeing 'Brahma' glance that only beauticians have. This 'Brahma' glance analyses your hair, body parts, weight, accessories, jewellery, the condition of your handbag and your footwear with one look.

What is always useful is my avatar of 'Please help me, I am a nice person. I have wandered in from the Harappan civilisation.'

'Yes, ma'am, what can we do for you?'

'I would like to colour my hair.'

'Of course. Do you have an appointment?'

'No, I suddenly decided to do it.'

'Of course, of course. Please have a seat.'

She and I looked doubtfully at the plush seats from which getting up in a dignified manner would be improbable.

'Ma'am, please have a seat here,' she said.

A nice plastic chair magically appeared.

'Steve, please help ma'am out.'

I baulked.

'Steve? You are assigning a male hairdresser?'

I then noticed a swarm of young men moving all over the place.

'Ma'am, we have only male staff.'

By this time, I had already been shifted to another chair in front of a huge mirror.

'Er ... I am not used to this. Please help me with a lady.'

By this time, Steve had walked up to me, picked up a fistful of my hair, and was examining it dispassionately.

Then he looked at me in the mirror and smiled.

He kneeled down so that he was on level with me.

'Ma'am, my mother wears a bindi like you! She is in my hometown, not with me.'

I smiled, comfortable with the Nirupa Roy imagery.

'What hair products do you use?'

'Meaning?'

'You know, what do you apply on your hair?'

'Oil!'

'You use hair oil?'

'Yes.'

'What oil?'
'Coconut oil.'
He winced. 'How many times a week?'
'Every day.'
'Any other hair products?'
'Like what?'
'Conditioner?'
'I have it, but I don't use it.'
'Which brand?'
'I don't know. It was a gift.'
He looked as though he would burst into tears on the spot.
'Hair wash?'
'Every day.'
'Ma'am, you need to first stop oiling your hair so much.'
'I can't.'
'Why?'
'I can't sleep at night without oiling my hair.'
He looked at me helplessly.
'Come with me.'
He took me by the hand and escorted me to a wall full of products.
'Ma'am, if you colour your hair, you will need to use special hair products for washing, conditioning, colour rinse plus hair oil massages.'
'How many times?'
'Regularly. Twice a month at least. Plus touch ups.'
'What's that?'
'Touch up of your hair colour once a month.'
'I can spare time for all this twice a year.'
He clasped my hand again.
'Why did you think of colouring your hair?'
By now he had become my on-the-spot counsellor.
I told him about the Aishwariya Rai ad.

'Ma'am, those colours are not even available here. They are imported and people pick them up when they go abroad. Do you travel often?'

'Up to Mahabaleshwar … yes.'

We laughed as he persuaded me to try a bottle of hair serum, did a step-by-step demonstration of how to use it, came with me to where my car was parked and escorted me back into my world while he made his way back into his.

Lockdown saw a lot of videos of Shilpa Shetty doing yoga and gardening. Impeccable living room, Shilpa Shetty stretching, her trainer smiling approvingly.

If I were to practise yoga, CP would be on one of his con-calls and visually supervising me. I have never seen him smile approvingly at me, so let's pass that. The sambhar would be bubbling on the stove and I would shriek, panting, 'Somebody, put off the gas!' The driver would pick up the keys and courteously enquire if I want something. '*Palak leke aaiye* (Get two bunches of spinach),' I would gasp. The istriwala would breeze in. '*Bhabhi-ji, Ramdev Baba ko try kijiye* (You must try Baba Ramdev).' The kids would be traipsing past me multiple times with cups of tea and coffee.

Another video shows Shilpa Shetty crouching down perfectly, her perfectly shaped hands with beautifully shaped fingernails sinking into the soil, perfect smile flashing. In modulated tones, she says, 'Today, I have four lovely brinjals from my own garden!' A perfect line of pots stretch in front of her, bringing to mind the famous rhyme:

> *Mary, Mary, quite contrary,*
> *How does your garden grow?*
> *With silver bells and cockleshells,*
> *And pretty maids all in a row.*

First, if I try to crouch like that, two of the kids would have to crouch behind me and hold my posterior firmly to ensure I stay upright. I would also need to have borrowed nail polish from Madhuri-ji, my neighbour, the previous night, and hastily coated it on my stubby fingernails. Between maintaining the position and sinking my non-existent nails into the earth, my voice would emerge in a piteous squeak.

Just this morning, while crossing Vashi on our way from Mahabaleshwar, I exclaimed, 'CP, let's stop at the Vashi vegetable market.'

CP, who was busy figuring out where we could stop for lunch, replied, 'Sangeetha, forget it. You have no idea how crowded it is. There is almost no space to walk. I used to go there for my mother because saving that extra ten rupees meant so much in those days.

'If I take you, we will first have to get a doli to lift you high up in the air, from which you would have to peep out and say, "I want this, I want that."'

The kids and I were rolling in mirth, imagining me in a doli, buying vegetables.

Sangeetha, you are quite contrary,
How DOES your garden grow?
What stories your potbelly would tell,
Of how you pant and yell,
How DO you keep your plants in a row?

Some are purple and gold flecked grey,
For she who has journeyed through life midway,
Whose hands have cherished, whose love has blest,
And cradled fair sons on her faithful breast,
And serves her household in fruitful pride,
And worships the gods at her husband's side.
            —*The Bangle Sellers* by Sarojini Naidu

I am forty-nine years old today. I feel seventy. I have aged. I look at my sixteen-year-old children and feel grateful that we have come so far. Somewhere in my corpulent frame, like a streak of silver that you spot on a vast mountainside, there is a waterfall of energy that propels me, that does not let me tire, that provides the nourishment of hope and determination to work, to think, to create, to foster, to not give up and to make something worthwhile.

CP got two tatty (they looked tatty even when new, so one can imagine how charming they are—and with stripes too!) T-shirts free, or something close to free, on sale a few years ago. He was so excited with his free T-shirts that he insisted on wearing them alternately during lockdown. Lakshmi is the only family member who is as devoted to these T-shirts as he is, and she insists he wears one of them after returning from work.

Before going to bed, Lakshmi keeps out clothes for me to wear the next day. She takes out Jayanthi's shoes for her and puts them away after their daily walk.

She waits for Jayashree to return from college and follows her around patiently with her nightshirt till she changes.

Krishna is home for the holidays, so she sleeps on the floor next to his bed and tucks her hand under the pillow on which he rests his head.

Krishna's moving out of home had a profound impact on her. When we went to Bangalore for the Diwali holidays and dropped him off at college, it was as if a coin had dropped for her: 'This is where he belongs.'

I moved fast and asked CP for help. We were returning to Mumbai that same night and I felt Lakshmi was ready for a big move and Jayanthi would definitely follow her lead.

'CP, please shift the bed out of Krishna's room and put the two single beds from the other room in there. Please get a picture taken of the room with the two single beds and give it to me.'

Tough and implacable as CP is, it is his willingness to walk the path with me as a parent that has kept us going. He understood that I was trying to do something and time was precious.

He called the office of the architect who had refurbished the house for us some years ago. Two people went to our home, dismantled the beds, manoeuvred them between one room and another, got the rooms cleaned, had the pictures taken and sent them to me

It was time to leave for the airport. Everyone was quiet and trying to smile. Krishna kept everyone's spirits up with his fund of foolish jokes.

This was the moment.

I spoke to Lakshmi. 'Lakshmi, Krishna is going to college. We are saying bye. We are going home.'

So saying, I showed her the pictures of the new sleeping arrangement.

'This is your bed. This is Jayanthi's bed. You will sleep here. Jayanthi will sleep here.'

After eighteen years, she was going to sleep in a room on her own, with Jayanthi, and without Jayashree or Krishna.

Lakshmi looked at me with big eyes.

'Okay,' she said and walked away.

I wondered what she had understood.

We reached Mumbai at 11 p.m. and it was past midnight before we got home, exhausted beyond words.

I had shown Lakshmi and Jayanthi the pictures several times by then and discussed the new sleeping arrangements with them.

Lakshmi changed into her nightclothes and stuck to her routine of taking out clothes for CP, Jayashree and me. She put away Jayanthi's shoes and went inside her room.

I was hanging around, trying to look busy and watching what she did.

She lay down on her bed. Jayanthi followed her lead and slept on the other bed.

That was it.

It was quiet and without any fuss at all.
I worried and worried.
What if they woke up and felt scared?
What if they felt the changes were too much for them?
Krishna has gone, Jayashree is not in the same room.

I tortured myself with the thoughts that could be running through Lakshmi and Jayanthi's minds.

I took a plastic chair and positioned it against the wall outside their room and slept sitting in the chair the whole night.

This way, I reasoned that I would get to know if one of them woke up and needed help.

At around 2 a.m., I cautiously entered the room and my heart melted. Lakshmi had put her pillow and bedsheets on the floor next to Jayanthi's bed and her hand was tucked under the pillow on which Jayanthi rested her head.

An imaginary conversation with St. Peter:

'Sangeetha, why should you be let into heaven? You are not disciplined. See how fat you are. I have to open both gates for you to fit in.'

'But see how much I tried. Dieting—2,154 diets. Walking. Kapalbhati. Have you ever tried giving up Thums Up?'

'Okay, Sangeetha, don't ask irrelevant questions. What other good have you done?'

'I've raised my children to be good human beings and managed to stay sane.'

'Sangeetha, every mother does that. What is different about what you did?'

'I have spent hours, days and years hiding vegetables and fruits from one child who has a chopping board and knife in her hand, protected remotes, mobiles, jewellery and other valuables from being thrown from the seventh floor balcony by a second child who looks like Gautam Buddha but behaves like Phoolan Devi, talked and laughed and cried with a third child who looks as light as a butterfly but carries the world's worries on her shoulders, raised the eldest child to be a gentleman at heart, a labourer by his hands and a thinking man with his mind.'

'Thinking a lot of ourselves, aren't we, Sangeetha?'

'Have you tried preparing for Ganesh Chaturthi while getting two children to draw, paint, cut and stick while trying to prevent Fevicol being squeezed out completely from the tube, while trying to prevent paper being systematically torn into pieces and quietly chucked under the table, after making endless rounds of tea, coffee, plus a full meal, after clearing the kitchen and combing the girls' hair to make them look less like bandits without guns and more like civilised human beings during lockdown?'

'Go back, Sangeetha. Take my car. I will let you in later. Don't forget to try and lose some weight.'

I was sitting in my room two days ago, in my big plastic chair—my favourite possession in this house after the dosa pan.

CP came to my room.

'I am not going to the office today.'

'Oh, why?'

'I've decided to take a break and relax.'

Ending this bold and brave declaration, CP drew the door closed. A primitive 'scrunch' sound emerged as the door handle came out in his hand.

Barely had his face started resembling the colour of the rising sun than the guilty party, Lakshmi, rushed in and grabbed the handle from him. She tried to twist it back inside the gaping hole in the door, gave up and handed it to CP.

'Help, Appa, help.'

CP, of course, spent the rest of the day doing two things:

1. Trying in vain to organise a carpenter to fix the handle.

2. Checking the doors to all the rooms. If Lakshmi had managed to yank out one handle, the others wouldn't be far behind.

The only advantage that has been bequeathed to me, which the rest of the family has realised, is this: Once I enter my room and close the door, nobody can open it from the outside.

CP placed the broken handle on a small table outside my room where it is displayed like a precious crystal vase. Whoever wants to come in has to pick up the handle, fit it into the gaping hole, twist it in while grunting and groaning, wait for a scrunching sound—'kachaku kachaku'—to emerge from the holy union between the door and the handle, then, wet with perspiration and glowing red with victory, gain entry into my room.

CP, of course, looks apoplectic every time he has to engage in the 'kachaku kachaku' activity in order to talk to me. The only other alternative is to stand outside the door to my room and shout.

Because everyone knows that I am not getting out of my big plastic chair.

I hope the door stays this way. It works to my advantage. Last I heard, CP had placed an order for five door handles, expecting a tsunami of dysfunctional doors.

I had just wrapped up the most significant of my household chores, which is dinner time, having successfully navigated the hurdles of, 'Amma, not baingan once again', 'Is the alu fry you made last Tuesday in the fridge?', 'Is it okay if I have fruit instead?', 'This curd looks weird', 'Are we never ever going to get pasta?'

Jayanthi does not say any of these things but sits at her plate with a saintly expression that actually means, 'Let me see how long I can make dinner last tonight and at what point Amma will start doing Zumba around me.'

After all this, I clear the kitchen, the most irritating task invented by god.

So I was pretty irritated by the time I entered my tiny room and parked myself in the largest plastic chair I could find in the market.

Maybe that's why I was so irritated to see Kareena Kapoor's irritating outfit in a video.

What WAS the contraption she was wearing? She stumbled, looked awkward and worse than how I look when I have to bend and serve food to elders at family functions while wearing my nine-yard saree.

I felt sorry for her.

What was that green cloth that wound itself around her like an abdominal belt that she does not need? (I am still looking for an abdominal belt that will fit me, but they say I have to lose weight in order to get the weight loss abdominal belt so you can imagine my predicament.)

This green abdominal belt then proceeded to fall in an untidy trailing heap on the floor, which she uncomfortably stumbled over before entering the set of the show *Dance India Dance*.

Who designs these clothes? They can first use me as a clothes horse.

Despite my ample proportions, I am quite dexterous thanks to years of practice with old-fashioned trailing dupattas and *Mughal-e-Azam*-style long kurtas that I gracefully manage with forty extra kilos on my frame. (My doctor almost prostrated himself before me. 'Just lose ten kilos, Mrs Chakrapani. You can't keep coming back looking the same. You ARE a lovely lady, but the kilos have to go.')

If they had tried the green abdominal belt with the trailing heap on me, I would have whacked the designer soundly on his posterior with my flat dosa ladle and told him to buzz off. Then Kareena Kapoor would have landed an outfit that lent her poise and grace—something she definitely deserves.

When we had our house renovated, my intellectual powers creaked to life and I delivered what I genuinely believe is a masterstroke.

CP's room had a small extension that was used as a study. I asked for it to be converted into a small room just for me. CP was not at all convinced. The architect, who by now was already struggling with my quaint and old-world ideas, argued that it would be impossibly small.

I stuck to my guns and when our home was finally ready, my room emerged as the most cosy, cute space. A space that CP frankly envied. So he walked in the day after we shifted. I was reading a book and looked up with my specs perched on my nose.

'I am the master of this house,' he said.

'Of course,' I replied.

'Everything here belongs to me.'

I blinked, this being a very new avatar of CP that I was seeing.

I replied, 'Ya, ya. Don't forget that the kitchen does not belong to you since only I know what to do with it.'

He did not look pleased with my observation but continued, 'So I have decided that this room belongs to me.'

I let out an outraged shriek and he carried on. 'In exchange for this room, I will give you my room with the double cupboard, study area, separate cupboard for files and documents, dedicated and attached bathroom, with French windows overlooking the park.'

I said somewhat smugly, 'No. I appreciate your kingly offer, but I am happy with what I have.'

Jayashree and Krishna have also made several openly jealous remarks about my room and tried to wrest it from me. Lakshmi contents herself with walking into my room every day and looking at the sarees that I have never worn (the ones I will wear after losing thirty-five kilos) and shouting, 'New, new.' The Buddha-like Jayanthi likes the fact that my room has fewer things in it and does not desire anything more than to sit there quietly.

It's now nearly a year since we moved. On a Sunday evening, you are most likely to see this scene: In my room, I will be in a chair, reading a book as usual. Lakshmi will be sitting on the floor, watching SRK. Jayanthi and Jayashree will be sprawled on my bed with gadgets of different kinds. Krishna will also be on the floor. A game of Scrabble may be going on, with the board dangerously perched atop the corner of the bed. CP, after completing his daily worship of the *Economic Times*, will wander in. One of the kids will scramble up to fetch him a chair. He will start watching SRK with Lakshmi. He and I will start a friendly argument about any topic under the sun. Some snack will be distributed amongst us all.

Unqualified bliss!

At such times, I realise that a home is truly defined not by space, not by furniture or colour coordination, or whether you have crystal adorning your table or an earthen bowl filled with whatever flowers you could find.

We may fight. We may argue. We may not talk to each other sometimes because we are so mad with each other. But if we have time, we want to spend it together. If there is a problem, we will try our best to solve it together.

That's the power that converts a tiny room into a comfortable, comforting and simple paradise.

I have always wanted to run an eatery. I even had the name decided: Sree Rama Hot and Fresh Idlis. Every time we take a holiday, our favourite activity is to discuss the hotel and its profitability threadbare. This time, we took a three-day trip to Prakriti Resorts at Kashid.

Lots of open space and buggies whisking people back and forth. CP was the last to get off the buggy and, as is his practice, he asked the buggy driver his name.

'Shukla,' the man smilingly replied.

'Thank you, Shukla-ji,' said CP, waving him away.

Over the next three days, Shukla-ji gave us an extra ride and we chatted with him about his family and his work schedule. Hailing from Uttar Pradesh, he has worked here for seventeen years and goes home during the off season. He had only good things to say about his workplace and employers.

Kashid was about moonlit skies, thick lines of trees and Shukla-ji's happy-go-lucky nature. CP and I felt more than a trace of envy as we said goodbye to Shukla-ji and his contented disposition.

I told the kids, 'Make sure you take a leaf out of CP's book. Drivers, waiters, helpers have names and if we don't bother to find out their names, the Shukla-jis of the world will pass us by.'

I achieved my lifelong ambition and made cutlets last night, thanks to the fact that CP is travelling and the job description of mealtime undergoes a drastic change every time he travels.

Lakshmi ambled over to the kitchen this morning and started foraging in the fridge.

'What do you want?' I asked.

'Vada,' she said.

'Oh,' I thought pridefully, 'she wants the amazing cutlets I made last night.'

She took out a microwave plate and put five on it.

Five!

Five cutlets!

Sometimes, just sometimes, mothers know when to shut up and not start bleating advice immediately.

So I shut up.

She warmed the cutlets, opened a drawer, took out another plate, transferred three cutlets to this plate and left two on hers.

Oh!

My heart swelled.

She had kept them for Jayanthi.

Who had not even woken up as yet!

Look at her unspoken love.

Taking out Jayanthi's shoes before a walk, giving her water to drink, holding her hand tightly when they go out.

Lakshmi's love is unique and wordless, speechless.

If Jayanthi cries, will Lakshmi hug her? No.

Will she comfort her? No.

Will she ask her, 'What happened, Jayanthi?' No.

Will she solve her problem? No.

Will she get help for Jayanthi? Yes.

Will she come and drag me to Jayanthi? Yes.

Will she make a noise and attract attention? Yes.

People with autism are magnificent, mysterious, surprising, complex, loving, caring, vulnerable, with hidden depths.

My ruby earrings went missing this morning. In an act of remarkable foolishness, I had stuffed my gold chain and ruby earrings into an empty coffee mug last night and kept it on the study table in my room.

This morning, the chain was there but the earrings were missing. I knew that my daughter, Lakshmi, was behind it. I did not have the heart to wake her up that early in the morning.

CP stepped in to help, with a grim expression at my weak 'Jewellery in the coffee mug' explanation. He had infinite faith in his younger daughter Jayanthi and started looking out of all the windows to see which one she had chosen to throw them down from. Then he crawled under the sofas, which is another favourite throwing spot for Jayanthi.

Finally, I placed the gold chain back in the coffee mug and woke Lakshmi up.

She followed me blearily to my study table.

'Tomato,' I said, pointing to the coffee mug with the chain. 'Where are my earrings?'

She looked at me with sleep-filled eyes.

Then, she turned around, opened the drawer under the mirror, scrabbled in it and produced a box, opened it and gave me my earrings.

CP was watching and I could read his thoughts.

'At least, it's my discipline—and not my wife's impetuousness—that has passed on to my daughters, thank heavens!'

I envy people who are not fat. Why? If there is one thing I envy, it is the ability to run.

I would love to be able to run. I am not talking about marathons and races. I am talking about running to the kitchen to turn off the stove before the milk boils over. Running to stop a door from banging shut loudly. Running to play with Jayanthi when she gambols like a deer in a park.

Have you ever seen a combination of a waddle and a whoosh? Well, that's what I do. I have perfected the technique of speeding my waddle and whooshing to reach a place quickly.

I also would love to slide a seat belt across the ample abdomen that I wish I could magically suck in. I don't hesitate to clearly ask for a seat belt extension when I am on a plane so I can make myself comfortable.

One evening, I was flying back to Mumbai and got a very good price on a Vistara flight (Rs 2,400!). It was a long and torturous route to my seat as passengers ahead of me lugged their hand luggage and effortlessly put the bags in the overhead compartment. Even if my girth was magically reduced, I could never reach the storage compartments above the seat.

I might as well have started singing loudly:

> *I am a little teapot, short and stout.*
> *I do have a tummy, but I don't have a pout,*
> *Please don't look aghast at my old-fashioned luggage as I wander about,*

I need your help to yank it up, without a doubt.

So I always check-in my baggage.

As I waited to find my seat, a slender and trendily dressed woman slid (I don't know how to slide into anything) into the seat next to mine. She was able to fit her bag next to her on the seat and slide the seatbelt across her stomach. I sighed with envy and plonked myself into my seat.

I tugged on either side to find the ends of the seat belt and simultaneously tried to catch the eye of an air hostess to ask for the seat belt extension. However, the belt kept extending and the latch comfortably clicked into place. I smiled like a cat that had got two bowls of cream.

Like the late Zakir Hussain proclaiming 'Wah! Taj!', I hailed the airline to myself. 'Wah! Vistara!'

Krishna says, 'If you want to wake up the entire building and all our neighbours simultaneously at six in the morning, get Lakshmi's blood test done.'

There is a blood collection centre representative whom we fondly call Blood Test Uncle, BT Uncle for short.

We have perfected a series of steps to prepare for blood collection.

First, BT Uncle spreads his wares at the dining table and Sai Baba vibhuthi is applied on the victim.

Then CP says in a falsetto tone, 'Okay, I am getting my blood test done.'

BT Uncle puts the black strap on CP's arm and the falsetto tone continues.

'See how I am smiling.'

'Nothing at all.'

CP looks at BT Uncle meaningfully till he puts the needle or whatever against CP's skin.

'Done, HA HA HA!'

'See how I am laughing.'

All this while Lakshmi and Jayanthi are gazing at us out of the corner of their eyes and then away again.

I say, '*Mera bhi kar dijiye* (Please do my blood test also).'

Then, since I firmly believe that the spirit of Meena Kumari resides in me, I give a more realistic rendition of blood test collection than CP, for which, when I celebrate my sixtieth birthday, the Dadasaheb Phalke Award for fat and hardworking mothers will be conferred upon me.

Then I utter small, realistic shrieks for a few seconds.

'Done, it's done.'

'Everyone, clap for Amma!'

This is the one time you can see CP participating enthusiastically.

Then Jayanthi comes for her turn, escorted by Jayashree and Krishna.

She squeals continuously, looks around with troubled eyes, we feel as if we are Medusa reborn and try our best to reassure her. Finally, CP growls, Jayanthi settles, the blood is collected and we clap feverishly till Lakshmi comes.

Lakshmi is our in-house Pele, Usain Bolt, Mike Tyson when it comes to asserting her rights vocally.

We look at her respectfully, look at each other, and position ourselves around her the way Dhoni would position his men on the last ball of an India–Pakistan match and India is bowling.

CP, in his anxiety and hurry to just finish it off, comes forward and grips her arm.

'No, no, wait,' I say and waggle my eyebrows at him.

'Don't restrain her now. Let her feel free.'

BT Uncle tells her in a singsong voice that he has perfected over the years and must be practising in his bathroom before he leaves for our place in the morning, 'Come, Lakshmi, come.'

'Good morning, Lakshmi.'

'*Strap dal diya*, very good (I've placed the strap, very good).'

'Yes, great,' we parrot enthusiastically.

This is the time Krishna looks anxiously at the clock and says, 'Come on, let's go for it and wake up the entire society at one go without a public address system.'

The moment the needle advances, Lakshmi utters a bloodcurdling yell. We all move in around her in one tight circle in which Blood Test Uncle tries valiantly to hold his own.

'*Ek minute jagah dijiye, nahin toh blood nahin nikal sakta hoon* (Please give me a little space to take the sample).'

We barely give him a few centimetres.

CP holds Lakshmi's arm in a Bahubali pose.

Jayashree and Krishna hold the other arm in a more compassionate manner, while I direct all the players.

'Hold shoulder and forearm,' I say, 'so she can't move.'

'Krishna, crawl underneath and hold her legs.'

Now we realise that Lakshmi has formed her own solution to getting the test done.

She continues shouting vociferously. Her arm remains in CP's grip on the table. But she slides under the table and sits on the floor. Still shouting, she allows Blood Test Uncle to draw blood, ensuring that she does not have to see it being done.

All of us look at the collected blood as if a bag of diamonds has just been harvested from the Kimberley mines. Perspiration is wiped off all our faces. Urmila, our morning helper, who has been bleating helpful suggestions from the kitchen that all of us have steadfastly ignored, makes her only contribution to the process.

She brings a cup of tea for Blood Test Uncle.

Though none of us have had any refreshment, though our lips are parched and though CP longs for his adhrak chai and I long for my Sunrise, we gaze at Blood Test Uncle admiringly as he savours his tea.

Then Lakshmi steals everyone's heart by fetching her tea and pulling up a chair next to Blood Test Uncle and drinking it companionably with him.

He finally gets up, says bye to Jayanthi who is in the furthermost corner of the living room from him, turns to Lakshmi, pats her head and says, 'Thank you, Lakshmi.'

'Thank you,' she patters back in the trademark autistic style without looking at him.

But he knows that a person with autism does not have to look at you to know that you belong.

By having a cup of tea with him, Lakshmi had extended an invisible hand of acceptance, trust and friendship.

Autism. There are many ways to connect with each other.

A few days ago, a temporary caregiver began staying with us 24/7. She had no previous experience of working with an autism family. The first thing she did was to hold Lakshmi and Jayanthi's arms to help them walk. She tried to feed them.

I explained, 'They eat and bathe on their own, exercise for ninety minutes a day, work and earn for their work. They enjoy singing, are learning to dance and they have their own phones.'

'Then why a caregiver?'

'They have phones but can only use some features on their own. For others, they need help. They go to work but need help to travel. At the workplace, Jayanthi needs reminders to use the washroom. They walk for one hour in the evening and thirty minutes after dinner, but they need a companion. Their communication is limited, so safety becomes an issue.'

People with autism can do many things and yet require support in others. Autism is complex and, like oxygen, permeates across every part of the individual, affecting overall functioning either mildly, moderately or more.

'Why are there pictures of bathing in the bathroom?'

'That's an organised visual reference for how to have a bath. Once a week, they wear a swimming costume and I enter the bathroom for a supervised bath.'

'Why a costume?'

'To protect their dignity and safety.'

'Why is the bathroom door open?'

'When the caregiver or I enter the bathroom with my daughter, the door cannot be locked. To ensure her safety. It's a protocol we have.'

'What are these pictures in their room?'

'It gives them an idea of the schedule for the day. Breakfast, work, rest, teatime, exercise, dinner and so on.'

'Why?'

'Planning helps my daughters be more prepared for their day and that helps self-regulation.'

'So you tell them everything in advance?'

'Yes, just like how you and I like to know what we are going to be doing.'

'But what if something new happens?'

'Oh, that happens every day! In fact, I ensure something new happens every day, for which there is no picture. That is called surprise management. To help them prepare for life.'

'Am I the only caregiver?'

'No. There are different kinds of caregivers. One who helps the adult with daily living skills. The parent or sibling or teacher or guardian is also a caregiver. These people help the person with autism to realise their best potential, identify challenges, manage and overcome challenges through life.'

Now, I turned the questioning around and asked her, 'What about you?'

'Me?'

'Yes. You. Tell me about your family, your boyfriend or your husband. Please share. Be happy. Eat well. Make friends with people here.

'Always remember that my daughters may not say much but their understanding of language is amazing. When you want to talk about them or any trouble you are having with them or you want to talk to your boyfriend, be out of their hearing.

'Give them their space and yourself some space too.
'Knock on the door.'
'What door?'
'Any door.'
'Meaning?'
'In your caregiving experience, you will see strange behaviours, you will encounter problems in caring. Sometimes you may get tired.
'At that time, go to the parent or the teacher or the supervisor.
'Help yourself. Help my child.
'What can my daughters do for you?'
'I do my own things. I don't need help.'
'I mean, how can they "care" for you?'
Blank look.
'Can they help you make your bed? Make you a cup of tea? Get you water?'
'I can ask your daughter for a glass of water?'
'Why not? Ask her the way you would ask a friend. When you give her a chance to care for you, it helps maintain equality.'

Caregiving for people with autism is complex. You may not get respect from such a person because of their behaviour challenges. But you will have to give respect and dignity. It is their right.

Caregivers for people with autism need training, supervision, support, and they also need 'care' from the community. That 'care' is the right of caregivers.

Krishna has always found it easy to say bye to me.

Bye, when I took his sisters from the NICU one by one while he waited fifty-four days for his turn.

Bye, on his first day at school: he could not walk then and had to be carried.

Bye, when he was a scrap of a baby and taken for his first surgery, which was followed by fourteen other surgeries.

The masked surgeon would stride out of the OT, hold out his arms and say, 'Mrs Chakrapani', and I would hand over the baby to him. He would march inside, Krishna's head wobbling and struggling to stay upright. With that wobbling head, Krishna would calmly look ahead and never back at me.

Before Krishna was sent home after his birth, the sonologist had examined his brain. 'You have given birth to an Einstein, don't worry,' he said.

Now, after eighteen years, Krishna wants to meet the sonologist and show him his maths paper. 'Please tell me what's happening here. Where is your Einstein?'

The ability to laugh at oneself is important in a family like the Chakrapanis. It is the only way to survive and also helps us handle CP.

'I broke the remote. So foolish of me, so clumsy of me, ha ha!'

Not that it helps divert CP's agitation away from the victim.

When CP and I went to Christ College in Bangalore for the first time, we were enchanted with the green expanse of the campus. We attended the parent orientation, saw Krishna being enveloped by a mass of youngsters and waited aimlessly till one of the professors told us to eat lunch and get back.

Krishna emerged finally and we were allowed to escort him to the hostel entrance and hand over the luggage. The guard told us firmly that the students would take their luggage up and parents can't help.

We watched with pride.

Our son, see! How nicely he is carrying all the luggage without making a fuss.

It was time for CP and me to leave and I was not ready. This time too, Krishna did the honours.

He took me by the arm, escorted me to the car. 'Amma, don't worry, I will WhatsApp you.' He patted me paternally on the shoulder, gently shoved me into the car, exchanged nods with his father, waved and walked away.

Without turning back.

Bye, Krishna.
Au revoir.
Until we meet again.

Krishna, he who was nicknamed Yanai papa (baby elephant) by the NICU sisters at Bombay Hospital while he waited to be taken home.

Every chair at home has a role to play. Lakshmi has a spacious yellow plastic chair that she keeps in front of the computer where she pays daily obeisance to Shah Rukh Khan.

Till a couple of years ago, if one of her siblings happened to be sitting in it, Lakshmi followed a very simple and effective form of evacuation. She would stand right behind the sibling and slide the chair out from under the posterior of the victim. The said person would sink noisily to the ground and Lakshmi would take over.

We successfully taught Lakshmi to shout, 'Get up'. She substituted it with, 'Shut up', no doubt influenced by Krishna and Jayashree's pristine language. CP was the unfortunate recipient of this communication, which I freely admit made me roll around in juvenile mirth.

We also have a rocking chair at home with a base of woven cane. CP found Lakshmi tugging vigorously at the cane. Much to CP's agitation, our part-time helpers began depositing washed and dried clothes on the collapsed cane chair. So he finally took the cane chair to be refurbished.

Apart from this, there is a ten-year-old sofa set in wood. The secret of its long life is:

1. It does not have any cushions and so you only sit on it when you are desperately tired and there is nowhere else to sit.
2. It is positioned opposite a TV that does not work and an audio system that only works after you crawl on the floor in close

imitation of Surya Namaskar step 5 and fiddle with a profusion of wires.

Therefore, there is no earthly reason for family members to sit there, which accounts for its longevity.

However, visitors to our home sink happily into it. Tea, coffee, something homely and tasty to eat are brought out.

That, in essence, is the job description of a chair. To offer instantaneous relief to a guest, make a person feel loved and welcome, fuel the heart with affection and the tummy with food. So the sofa without cushions, without a working TV and with an eccentric audio system, still does its job.

Athithi devo bhava.

Velu was the caretaker of my parents' small and beautiful beach-facing home in Chennai. One morning, Appa was in the garden when he saw a long snake sliding inside and around the house.

Having worked in the agriculture industry, travelled the country extensively, addressed farmers in villages at the tea shop and addressed corporate events with equal ease, Appa is down to earth, sturdy, affable and straight talking: a true officer and gentleman.

Appa knew that Amma was petrified of snakes. He had no choice but to warn her. Amma unhesitatingly bolted for her room and locked the door.

Appa yelled for Velu to start finding and chasing the snake that had gone into hiding behind a clump of bushes near the entrance.

Velu looked supremely unconcerned and masterfully summoned his wife: 'Chinamma! Chinamma! Bring the camphor!'

After lighting a small pile of camphor on the base of a long stick, Velu held it in front of the bushes and what he fondly imagined was the snake.

As Appa watched in growing disbelief, our man addressed the snake:

> '*Na yena thappu panen* (What mistake have I made)?
> '*Na onaku thappu panena* (Have I ever harmed you)?'

Appa brought the one-sided dialogue to an abrupt end.

'Velu, will you please explain *briefly* what is going on? My wife will not come out till the snake is evacuated. Chase it out right now!'

Velu looked on disapprovingly, remarkably poised for a man with a snake behind a clump of bushes on one side of him and a formidably angry Appa on the other.

'Saar!' (In Tamil, we don't know how to pronounce 'sir'; we like to elongate it to show our genuine respect, so we say 'saar' to rhyme with not only 'car' but 'caaaar'.)

'Saar,' said Velu, 'I know how to send the snake out. I have driven out so many snakes in my village.'

With Appa hopping helplessly and impatiently from one foot to another, Velu more or less forced him to listen to the story of the last snake that he had evacuated from his village.

'Saar, I showed the karpuram (camphor) and asked, "Did I do you any harm?"'

'The snake shook its head from left to right three times. Then I asked the snake, "*Thiripi varuviya nee? Sathyam pannu* (Don't come back. Promise me)."'

'The snake nodded yes three times and went away.'

Barely had he finished than Appa told him with great civility that those were village snakes and these were urban dwellers and needed to be handled differently.

Velu then prodded the bushes a few times till the snake slithered outside our house in search of greener pastures.

Appa went in search of Amma and bleated through the gap in the firmly shut window, 'Mythili, come, the snake has gone!'

Like Velu, my mother did not respond to my long-suffering father.

'Chinamma,' my mother called through a gingerly opened window.

The now famous Chinamma appeared.

'Has the snake truly gone?'

Like the snake in Velu's story, Chinamma nodded three times.

Amma approached Velu gratefully till Appa firmly intervened lest the story of the nodding snake be recounted.

'Mythili, Mythili! What mistake have I made? Can I not get a cup of tea?'

Mystified, my mother obliged and, seated once more in their garden and over a pot of tea, my father allowed Velu to tell my fascinated mother the story of the nodding snake.

Three times.

Krishna and Jayashree are presently reading *Lochinvar* at school, and the poem still mesmerises me the way it did many years ago when I was a schoolgirl.

If I were to transport *Lochinvar* to a Tamilian wedding right now, CP, bless him, would have the gumption to ride a horse, but I would be in no position to be swung up unless the horse had a sidecar tied to it like a buggy.

I could then (somewhat) gracefully get into it, wearing the requisite nine-yard saree for my wedding. I still faithfully don my nine yards a few times a year so that part of it should come easily.

My dad would never—not even in his dreams—prevent us from riding away since he believes the sun rises and sets with CP. My mom would shower petals from her heavenly abode. My sister, who shares my irreverent sense of humour, would laugh uproariously.

Krishna, who considers himself more mature than me, would brush it off as a temporary phenomenon and settle down to wait for us to come back. Lakshmi, who loves horse rides, would try to climb onto the horse with CP, simultaneously shouting, 'Get down, get down.' Jayashree, my Girl Friday, would urgently ask me if there was food at home and whether she should serve her siblings. Jayanthi would be totally unaffected by the hullaballoo and watch us with saintly calm, perhaps thinking, 'These people are crazy.'

The question is, where would we go? It would be a bit difficult to elope with four kids and there would be no fun if we were not being chased. Plus, I am trying to imagine persuading CP to ride a horse with a buggy attached to it. He would then elope, but only with the horse.

One day, in around 2018, when the children were in Class VIII, CP returns home after meeting Krishna and me at the hospital and sees an animal rescue ambulance parked squarely in the middle of the building compound, with the rest of the Chakrapani family clustered around it.

The ambulance driver says, 'Your wife asked us to pick up a badly injured kitten in your building. We are treating it on the spot, but please keep the kitten overnight. We will come and pick him up tomorrow afternoon.'

CP is composed but aggrieved. 'We are managing three kids without you and now this kitten. I will ask the watchman to keep an eye on him till tomorrow.'

I subtly threaten him. 'The watchman has to guarantee that the kitten will not crawl away. Plus, crows may attack the kitten, so the watchman has to be alert. Plus, he must keep the kitten warm.'

CP interrupts me, 'Forget it. I will take the kitten home.'

I instruct Jayashree to suitably introduce the kitten to Lakshmi and Jayanthi. I call our helper before she leaves and request her to place the kitten in a cardboard box lined with newspaper and rags, and position it in such a way that I can monitor the kitten via CCTV.

I wait for CP to consume his dinner and request him to feed the kitten. He is not amused with the CCTV surveillance of the kitten.

Next morning, I call CP, and he sarcastically enquires, 'The kitten refused milk this morning. Do you want me to wait till his mood changes or may I have my tea in the meantime?'

I just called the animal rescue centre. The kitten is recuperating. Praise god and CP!

'CP, I want a house.'

'Okay.'

'An independent house.'

'Oh!'

'It should have a large, sprawling kitchen where I can cook to my heart's content.'

'Continue.'

'At least five rooms so that family and friends can drop in and stay over without a thought.'

'Hmmm.'

'A big garden in the front and another at the back. In front, there should be a big tree with a circular platform around it where I can sit and read in the afternoons. There should be fruit trees—chikoo and mango are a must—and I will have two dogs, Beauty and Blackie.'

'Oh, you've been planning this so well that you've named the dogs?'

'Yes, yes. I will have a kitchen garden at the back of the house so neighbours can drop in and pluck whatever they want.'

'Wow!'

'Most important, there should be a stone bench on either side of the entry to the main house (what we call thinnai in Tamil) and elephants (yanai) next to the thinnai.'

'Live elephants?'

'No, no. Stone elephants.'

'Errr … Where will this house be?'

'Oh, anywhere. I don't mind Bombay but I prefer a small town, actually.'

'And where will the children go for college, work and so on?'

'Oh, they would have settled by then.'

'Oh!'

'The most important thing is, coming back to the thinnai and yanai, I will sit there in the morning after coffee, etc., and clean rice, grams, etc. At that time, the lady in the neighbouring house should also be sitting at her thinnai and we will chat in a leisurely manner.'

At this point, CP's eyes bulge and in that so familiar sarcastic voice, combined with amazement over an illogical mind—of the kind of, 'Of all the nuts in the country, why did this specimen have to land up in my life?'—says, 'Sangeetha, I will definitely work on the thinnai and so on, but I can't ensure that your neighbour will clean rice at the same time as you.'

Yesterday afternoon, we returned from the briefest namesake of a holiday to Nashik. Replete with satisfaction from a massive breakfast, the kids and I lay like a mother and her puppies in the car, with the sun gently beating down upon us. CP spotted a long stretch of tomato fields and excitedly (if you can imagine CP as anything other than his imperturbable self) told the driver to stop. He briskly got down, fully expecting me to be right behind him.

I sat back and manifested an excited expression, thinking I could get away with it. Seeing 'The Look', I scrambled out and of course got genuinely excited to be among hundreds of tomato plants, bulging with green and red fruit.

The children refused to budge till CP gave a friendly yell to our driver to do something. Our driver, Sanjay, realised that a civilised approach would not work and started beating the sides of the car and making sounds similar to those herders use for cattle, sheep, etc. '*Hai, hai, niklo bahar* (Come on, get out)!'

Soon, the children tumbled out.

After a long chat with the farmers, we asked for two kilos of tomatoes. Then we asked for another kilo for Sanjay and they readily filled up our bag.

Much to our amazement, they refused to accept money. They smiled. 'The land belongs to everyone. We never sell directly from here. We sell only after the vegetables reach the market.'

I asked them, 'So many more people must be stopping here, right?'

One of them said, 'Yes, we give away boxfuls of tomatoes.'

Stunned by their generosity, I struggled for a way to express our feelings till CP and I remembered the bags of snacks in the car. We brought out the entire lot. A warm handshake of friendship and we were on our way, made wiser by the experience.

CP: 'Sangeetha, what are you making?'

My dad: 'Make paruppu urundai kozhambu.'

One could almost hear the trumpets roaring and drums beating.

'Why not?' I said. 'Everyone is at home. Eight of us should be able to do justice to it.'

Though I have made paruppu urundai kozhambu a few times, a search on YouTube was mandatory. Satisfied with my research, I began preparation.

Paruppu urundai kozhambu is a rich, flavourful and elaborate sambhar that is the ultimate test of a matriarch's culinary journey. The preparation of the kozhambu involves soaking and grinding toor and chana dals, tossing the paste in a little oil, making round balls, steaming them like idlis and ever so gently popping them into the bubbling sambhar and letting them swirl away before putting off the flame.

I positioned myself at the table opposite the kitchen as different members of the family moved in and out.

'Don't touch the sambhar vessel!'

Krishna: 'Why?'

'I've made paruppu urundai kozhambu.'

'Oh, that round vada wala sambhar?'

'Yes.'

'Wow!'

'You are making coffee?'

Jayashree: 'Yes, Amma.'

'Don't touch the sambhar vessel.'

'Why?'

'I've made paruppu urundai kozhambu.'

'Oh, that ball ball wala sambhar?'

'Yes.'

'Wow!'

Jayanthi wafted in like a deer in search of an apple, sniffed delicately at the sambhar and trotted away.

Lakshmi, who loves vadas, looked hopefully at the dumplings in the sambhar and went away, appeased. 'So many of them, surely I will get at least three or four?'

Finally, lunch was ready. Tiny alu fry, beans with coconut, minutely chopped cucumber pachadi (raita), fresh mango pickle (made that morning) and hot rice were on the table. The sambhar made its stately entrance and the karandi (ladle) was dipped into the vat, the dumplings delicately scooped up and rolled onto Appa's plate.

My father nodded like the king of the jungle. 'The urundais (dumplings) are intact and not crumbled, Sangeetha. How did you manage it with so many of them?'

I looked wise and tried not to look superior.

CP was on a call and came to the table with his head plastered to the phone on one side, picked up a plate, served himself the boring red rice that he eats every day, for which he deserves a medal, and scooped up the sambhar. The dumplings looked like red gold treasures on his plate. He was appreciative enough to look at me with the admiration that he last showed me when I found my debit card and he did not have to block it for the third time.

As soon as lunch was done and with singularly unseemly haste, both Appa and CP looked at me putting away the leftover sambhar into my precious Tupperware dabba and shouted, 'Keep it carefully. Keep it in the fridge for tomorrow.'

By tomorrow, this sambhar would have soaked in its multiple flavours, the urundais become more golden, more soft, more flavourful, tasting like something from the court of Indra.

Bright cardboard stockings with all our names put up in the living room, a Christmas star in the form of a rangoli adorning the entrance to our home, and paruppu urundai kozhambu.

Christmas, Tamil Iyengar style!

The queen was standing on the 300th floor of the palace, was wearing a diamond, was pushed, and her diamond fell from her crown and died!

I was wondering what rangoli to make, but I needn't have bothered. My lovely children provided the inspiration.

We were discussing how to write an autobiography and plotted the lives of a teacher, a singer and finally, a diamond. We went through the usual ritual of how the diamond was mined, sparkled bewitchingly, was stolen, was rescued, etc., till Krishna decided that the diamond landed up with Mukesh Ambani. Jayashree added fodder by saying that Ambani gifted it to the queen.

I then asked them to conclude the story. Jayashree, in her inimitable English, blithely said, 'Oh the queen dropped the diamond by mistakely and it fell down and died.'

I said, 'No, that's not possible. It would not have broken. Try again.'

She persisted. 'It fell from a height, Amma, and it died. Why can't you understand?'

I proclaimed in great style (if you can imagine a rotund and homely James Bond), 'No, because diamonds are forever.'

By this time, Krishna was losing patience and, clutching his hair, said, 'Arre, the queen was on the 300th floor of her palace and somebody pushed her from behind, she managed to save herself but the diamond fell down and died. Are you happy?'

The first place CP and I went to, after my father fell in love with him and after my parents were aghast when I said, 'This man is scary and I am better off as I am now,' and after my mother prayed like a Hindi film mother that I see sense and after two years when I told CP, 'Okay, but I like animals and I like books and I can do many inconvenient things like when the train is about to leave the station and slowly moving out, I will be at Higginbotham's trying to buy a book, I am that kind of person and I will marry you,' and after he gravely thanked me, was Munnar, in 2002.

CP's friend met us at the railway station and took us to his family home at Thrissur.

They are four siblings with four homes on a common piece of land. When we reached the place, many of the family members came out to meet us. With an easy casualness, they took us into each of their homes. Simple homes, with many of them deeply engaged with music, art and literature.

Finally, we visited the fourth bungalow and we were further enchanted. The prayer room in this home was large, with a sanctum closely resembling a temple, and it beckoned me with an intensity that I could not resist.

A whole group of young people from the ages of five to twenty-five from each of the four homes walked in quietly. Some in school uniforms, some in casuals. Each individual quietly sat at the altar, got up, went to the grandmother, touched her feet and left.

The grandmother, a serene and radiant lady, explained, 'We each have our own homes and kitchens. We pray together here and the young ones come and meet me before they start their day.'

What a joy. What a beautiful life.

To respect each other's space.

To be there for one another.

To go to your cousin's house and ask, 'What has Athai made to eat? My mother has made boring food today.'

To cry at your grandmother's feet that things didn't work out.

To tell an uncle, 'Please, will you teach me music?'

To burst into celebration at a birth or a wedding.

To grip each other's hands tightly and spend sleepless nights together dealing with loss and learning to embrace life again.

I was thirty years old, CP forty, and the impact of the visit to this family on both of us was profound. We loved their home, we loved their easy warmth and simple, nourished lives.

We did not know that the great lord watching was going to bless us with four beautiful and unique children.

The grandmother's kind and wise face has been a beacon for me as had it been, no doubt, for CP too.

We can't teach unity or love or acceptance through discourses or in the form of pills at bedtime, hoping our children will stand by each other. Both CP and I have tried to show it through our actions.

By saying sorry when one of us has made a mistake.

By being loving and respectful to our siblings.

By sharing the stories of our parents and their parents.

Twenty-one years have passed since Munnar. We are on our way to achieving that dream.

A happy family. Not perfect. Not in sync all the time. Not laughing and smiling all the time. But there for each other.

All the time.

Jayashree: 'Amma, there's very little sabzi for the night.'

Me: 'Om namo Swiggy!'

Jayashree: 'Okay.'

Me: 'Will you make dal? There is moong dal in the cooker.'

Jayashree: 'Ya, ya, I will make it. What should I do?'

Me: 'Keep green chillies, coriander, lemon, salt …'

Jayashree: 'Tell me the recipe, na. I will figure out and take out the ingredients.'

Me: '… haldi, hing powder, and the dal is ready.'

Jayashree: 'Continue. Continue.'

Me: 'Put the kadhai on the stove, put one spoon oil, don't keep it on maximum flame or minimum.'

Jayashree: 'Okay, go on.'

Me: 'Then take green chillies, chop them neither fine nor big. Remember to wash your hands afterwards.'

Jayashree: '*Jaldi bolo* (Tell me quickly)!'

Me: 'Once the oil is hot, but remember it should not be smoking hot …'

Jayshree: 'Forget it. You make it.'

Me: 'Aiyyo, aiyyo, sorry come back. Put the green chillies in the hot oil and let them change colour slightly. Add the cooked moong dal. Remember to hold the kadhai with the idikki.'

Jayashree: 'What's that?'

Me: 'Pakkad, pakkad.'

Jayashree: 'Okay.'

Me: 'Otherwise the kadhai may topple off the burner.'

Jayashree: 'Amma, I am eighteen!'

Me: 'Let the dal bubble. Add salt, haldi, hing. Turn off the gas, add chopped coriander. Cool slightly. Cut a piece of fresh lemon. Don't use leftover lemon.'

Jayashree: 'As if you are some five star chef!'

Me: 'I am no less. Wait till you taste it. You will fall at my feet.'

Jayashree: 'Okay, okay. Don't get excited!'

As she moved out of my room, I added, 'This is Paati's favourite, Jayashree. The way she would arrange everything on a plate before cooking! It would look so appetising that you would want to eat it even if you normally did not like that item. She used to make a simple tomato sabzi that Vaidehi Periamma and I are not able to make the same way. We've tried so many times.

'This dal she taught me when I was in the tenth standard.

'From her to me and from me to you.'

Jayashree and I looked at each other for a few seconds. No words were needed.

The dal was wonderful last night!

Where would we be without these invisible heirlooms?

Yesterday, I told the children, 'I wish someone would invite us to a birthday party.'

Not the new-age ones, where an entire restaurant is booked and there is an event consultant and customised gifts.

We have two young adults with autism who enjoy the purana zamaana birthday party.

A big chocolate cake. Lots of elders and children. Paper plates with a heap of chips and one samosa each. Water bottle for the return gift.

Yesterday, the children and I went for lunch to Cream Centre, Juhu. Lakshmi flipped through her AAC menu card and reeled off around twenty-five items that she wanted. We brought her down to Mother Earth and said that every person can choose one item. Finally, she settled for French fries.

Around twenty-five children and four mothers traipsed in and made themselves comfortable in one corner of the restaurant. Within minutes, the 'Happy Birthday' song rang out to a drum roll beat. Lakshmi went into a paroxysm of excitement. The eagerness on her face, the excitement in her eyes! She would have made a dash for their table, if not for our inhibiting presence.

That's the unpredictability of autism.

Something in her expression wrung our hearts and I said, 'How nice it would be if someone invited us to a birthday party.'

Jayashree: 'Forget it. Even when they were small, they were left out. Now, who will invite them?'

That was true. They were not excluded explicitly but very gently. The first exclusion was traumatic for all four children. I held several sessions with the children to help them understand that it was okay to go to a party without each other.

Then as they grew older, the texture of parties changed. Teenagers don't cut cake anymore. Chips and samosas are out. They take their friends out for a treat. Lakshmi and Jayanthi's concept of a birthday party has remained the same.

When the autism diagnosis comes in, at first the world is a lonely place. Your child with autism is a stranger whom you must befriend, understand, laugh, cry and work with together, till you finally hold hands and walk through life.

Gradually, your world becomes bigger with fellow parents of people with autism, teachers, therapists, neighbours, psychiatrists, counsellors, writers, thinkers, philosophers and even the relatives who once said, 'She has strange children,' but now say, 'They've grown so well.'

Yes, the autism journey is sometimes lonely and painful but as our children grow older, fellow parents fly down over our nests, cluck with empathy, drop nuggets of wisdom, share our journeys and invite us to birthday parties.

Some years ago, CP and I were at a jewellery store, adhering to our lifelong policy of not taking the brood along while shopping. This, we had discovered to our peril, was the only way out, unless we wanted to entertain the storekeeper by yelling at the kids or searching for them or showing them the way to the washroom. So we decided that unless we employ a shopping therapist, which CP says will effectively take us into an exalted league, we will shop by ourselves.

CP feels the shopping therapist's day will begin with first asking us, 'What are the things you are searching for?' Since we spend a large part of our waking hours searching for our possessions and suspecting each other of having taken them, our list is long, consisting of shoes, socks, charger, the mobile phone, hankies, spoons, and not to mention our star performer, Jayanthi. After searching for all these things, the therapist will take us shopping.

In fact, a very well-dressed woman had applied for a job at our place. After sniffing at my tatty appearance (as usual) and confirming that I *was* the lady of the house, she quoted an astronomical figure while stating that she had previously been employed with Shah Rukh Khan. I very kindly told her that as of now, CP has not yet got a role in the movies (the future too did not look too bright given his winsome personality) and I definitely did not qualify, before I escorted her out.

So, as I was saying, we were at a jewellery store and could not help noticing a young couple struggling to control their toddler in order to get her ears pierced. We waited and waited and finally moved in unison by unspoken agreement and offered to help. We requested the staff to move away, asked the mum to hold the toddler, CP held the head of the toddler, I grasped the shoulders and knees, the ears were pierced in about forty seconds. We shrugged off the waves of gratitude, completed our shopping and left.

If wishes were horses, our entire family would ride.

A year or two ago, our occupational therapist strongly recommended horse-riding therapy. Convinced that this would be the golden key to our bright future, I started campaigning with CP who, after more than a decade in my serene company, knew he had to do something to ensure a somewhat peaceable coexistence.

The horse therapist could give us only Sunday morning, which is a sacred 'So what if we have quadruplets, we can still drink coffee for two hours with all the newspaper editions that Mumbai offers and not go out at all' kind of time. But CP and I convinced ourselves that we could do this for the betterment of our family and the glory of our nation. So we galvanised our battalion and got into the car higgedly-piggedly.

The horse therapist looked dashing, the ground had seen better days, our children were more or less civilised, Jayanthi promptly disappeared, was promptly sought and bawled out by CP, and all was well with the world.

This is what ensued.

A couple of film stars wandered in and the therapist smugly let us know that he really rates.

Krishna, who has no clue about his lack of physical prowess, asked excitedly if getting a role in films can get easier with horse-riding skills.

CP affectionately told him to shut up and asked the horse therapist for five sessions a week.

Things started getting interesting after this point. Something in us, as unlikely as it sounds, appealed to the therapist.

He told CP, 'Sir, *itne session ke liye time nahi hai. Aap kya karo, mere se ek ghoda le lo* (Sir, I don't have time for so many sessions. But do one thing: take a horse from me).'

CP baulked.

'*Ek poora ghoda* (An entire horse)?'

I was stunned that the therapist could trust us so completely by handing over a horse to us. What if we ran away with it?

Krishna said pityingly, 'But, Amma, he knows you are not in a position to run at all, forget running away with the horse.'

By this time, I was in a fervent discussion with the therapist myself. He said, 'Just keep it tied up in your building.'

I passionately argued against tying up the horse and said meditatively, 'Maybe we can convert one of our parking areas into a paddock.'

Jayashree immediately wanted to know what is a 'paduka'.

Krishna said, 'Stupid, it's not paduka, it's a paddock.'

I said, 'The horse will need exercise. I will take it for morning walks after my prayers,' and I looked speculatively at CP. 'You can do the night walk after office. You can probably ride also. It will be very relaxing.'

Krishna said, 'Lakshmi will take care of the horse's food, Jayanthi and Jayashree will be its friends, and I will protect it from any harm.'

CP's expression, as he looked at us, was a combination of amazement at our stupidity and outrage at our instant acceptance of the idea itself. He quickly established control ('The Look', remember?), threw an arm over the therapist's shoulders and took him away from our evil influence.

The therapist came back sadder but wiser.

CP advised me, 'You know those plastic horses at Infiniti Mall? Please tell your therapist that it is all our family is fit for.'

I asked Krishna to send me a picture of his meal at the hostel. He replied, 'Are you serious?'

Then I threatened him with all kinds of dire maternal repercussions and he obliged. I opened my WhatsApp to check the picture and saw a kind of semicircle formation. I clicked on it and was happy to see Krishna's meal of roti, sabzi and dal.

At that moment, my phone rang. I spoke and went back to analyse the picture and what my son is eating. The picture was gone! I pressed that spot in vain. Nothing happened.

Then I roped Jayashree in and explained, 'The picture is gone.' She laughed, pinched my cheek and said, 'It's called "view once". Do you also want the app?'

Bewildered, I asked, 'Why would I want it?'

She said, 'If you want to send a picture that can't be reused or sent to anyone else, you use this feature.'

Imagine the world our young people are growing up in, where they are constantly inventing ways of securing their safety and privacy.

I've had many discussions with Krishna and Jayashree about how to deal with infringement and in how many ways they should be conscious about not infringing on others. It is not funny to take a person's picture, however close he may be, without permission. It is not funny to circulate a picture or a video of a person without permission. It is not wise to say or do some things on camera even if the person asking you to do it is your husband or boyfriend or wife or girlfriend or partner or soulmate or whatever is the technically right word to describe that person in your life.

Keep your clothes and common sense on, when the camera is on.

Simple.

If someone still infringes upon your rights, hurts you, humiliates you, scars you, don't give up. Pick up the phone. Call me. Call your father. Call your teacher or your mentor or a family friend.

Take help.

Untwist your shamed neck from the coils of anguish, put eye drops of fortitude in your reddened eyes, stretch your body in the infinite Surya Namaskar, straighten your back, face the world and start all over again.

Social media has become a complex world by itself and the time has come to introduce, explain and administer a Hippocratic 'social media' oath to ourselves, this generation and future generations to come.

First, do no harm.

One might wonder that after running a home for nineteen years in Mumbai, of which eighteen years have been with quadruplets, how many umbrellas would I have accumulated.

CP has always found it a source of anxiety, frustration and amazement that he is married to a woman who loves to give away umbrellas.

I look out for deals—buy one umbrella, get one umbrella free; buy two umbrellas, get one umbrella free, and as CP sarcastically culminates, buy all the umbrellas in town, free or otherwise. Then, unasked, I give umbrellas to our drivers, helpers and security guards and keep a stock at home of five extra umbrellas for people who visit but have forgotten to carry an umbrella.

CP: 'Sangeetha, by the way, where is the umbrella with the horse head that you insisted on buying?'

'I gave it to Chapati aunty yesterday.'

'WHAT? You could not find a saada umbrella to give her?'

'No, there were none left, but I will take it back from her today.'

'Here.'

'What's this?'

'A saada umbrella. Don't just take it back from her. Give her one in exchange.'

'My, my, you are also giving away umbrellas!'

'Sangeetha, I know what it is to not have an umbrella! My father could not afford to get even a saada umbrella. He would buy the long, purana zamana ones. When I was in the ninth standard, he finally got me a folding umbrella, the kind you could actually put inside a school bag.'

I called the kids and made them listen to the story of CP's umbrella.

'This is an inspiring story. Here is a man who is helping give away umbrellas today. Here is a man who has created an umbrella of hope, by making space for adults with special needs to work and learn in safety and comfort.'

The first rainfall of the monsoon is a day I get really excited about. I call the whole family to the terrace to stand in the rain. The children like to get wet while I close my eyes and look upward. I no longer pray for the rain to wash the autism in our family away.

I no longer shed tears that mingle with the glimmering raindrops on my face. I no longer beg, 'Make Lakshmi and Jayanthi normal.'

Nineteen years of rainfall in Mumbai have brought acceptance, gratitude, courage and the willingness to walk along with and work with autism like an old friend and a beloved troublemaker.

Here's to creating more umbrellas—saada, sturdy and dependable for our fellow beings, with and without autism.

Do CP and I know how to give a party?

Yes, with huge plates of medu vadas, tomato chutney and coconut chutney, hot rice, small onion sambhar, tiny potato fry, and a huge bowl of cucumber and tomato raita with green chillies and pomegranate seeds vying for supremacy over your taste buds.

Our guests have to fend for themselves because I stick to the kitchen, making vadas hot and fresh while CP makes last-minute dashes to Pooja Stores to get Thums Up, Fanta and Tropicana juice. Our friends make their way noisily to the kitchen and helpfully pass food along to others.

People divide themselves between our ancient unbreakable wooden sofa and the biggest dining table we could find at Pepperfry.

Lakshmi takes a great big blanket, covers herself with it from neck to toe, and takes up a corner of her bed, peaceably watching her peers from whom the great wall of autism—taller, heavier, thicker and more impenetrable than the Great Wall of China—separates her. Jayanthi sits like an island right in the middle of these peers, playing games on her tab, looking like one of them but not at all one of them.

Can Lakshmi lie down like this when we attend a wedding reception? Certainly not. Will she wait patiently while we go through the social niceties of greeting, chatting and finally eating, followed by more chatting before leaving for home? Yes, as long as we don't take undue advantage of her patience.

Greetings: One to maximum five minutes.
Chat: Three to fifteen minutes.
Eat: Up to twenty minutes.
Very good food with lots of desserts: Thirty minutes.
Chat again: One and a half minutes.
Gratefully leave for the parking lot and get into car: Two minutes.

What happens if things get delayed and we stay longer than Lakshmi's social bandwidth allows?

The same as what will happen to us if we are blindfolded and escorted to a German or Russian family's home for a get together. We can't see anything of interest, we don't have a thing to say to the people there. We only wonder *where* the food can be, and whether we can please eat and leave.

However, most autism parents are gifted with wonderful friends whom we can visit freely.

Where Lakshmi can make herself comfortable and is helpfully given a big blanket to lie down with.

Where Jayanthi can go to the washroom every hour.

Where people know that one vegetable has to be pressure cooked for Jayanthi to enjoy her food.

Where Lakshmi is lovingly told, 'Beta, no more chips. Wait for some time. *Khana milega sabko* (In a little while, we will all get food).'

Where Jayashree, Krishna, CP and I can spend time peacefully without turning our heads from side to side like well-trained and oiled pendulum clocks.

Yes, we know how to party autism style.

Good food. Zero formalities. Complete acceptance.

When CP and I travelled together, at least four people on the airport shuttle bus stood up and offered us their seats.

Both of were taken aback by this mass outpouring of concern, but both of us manfully stood.

There is no question that we have aged. CP sports a bald look these days, which makes him look more charmingly daunting than before, if that is possible.

I had coloured my hair only once in the past, tempted by the words 'deliciously brown shade that will make you fall in love again and again' or some such Mills & Boon slogan.

Both CP and I had enrolled in the quadruplet military academy as lifetime coaches in 2004 and share a camaraderie that does not require hair or hair colour to appreciate each other's worth. But anyway, I went ahead with the hair colour and when I was asked to admire my reflection in the mirror, I felt a lot of things remained unchanged.

My eyes were the same—a tangled mix of sadness, optimism and laughter. My heart felt the same—a bit tired but resounding with determination and energy. My walk remained the same—a bit unsteady after falling three times but measured, clamping down on the ground with every step, and ready to walk on and on.

So, as the hairdresser encouraged me to use a colour wash, a post-colour conditioner and oil serum, I asked myself, why am I doing this?

My greys and whites are testimony to the cobbled path I have walked, the number of falls I have endured, the number of potholes I have avoided, the amount of sunshine and rain that have soaked me again and again.

There was a long walk from the flight to the terminal building. When we got to the building at last, a buggy driver paused courteously. Both of us reacted with alacrity and jumped in.

Taking help is also part of this journey. Where would we be today, without the help and support we have been bolstered with over the years, the parents we've called and wept to, the therapists who've told us that this too shall pass, the neighbours who've understood our strange ways, and the family members who have loved us and loved us and loved us?

Yes, we have been on this buggy ride with many people, and we are where we are because of them.

Yesterday was CP's birthday. I followed the time-honoured tradition of buying gifts for him from each member of the family and return gifts from CP to each one of us. CP has a healthy respect for credit card bills and his face paled as the kids dragged in the huge blue bucket that is normally used to store water in emergencies. The bucket overflowed with parcels and I announced, 'I have not wasted money on unnecessary things this year as I did not have time to go shopping. As you open each Amazon parcel, I will tell you whether it is a gift for you or if it is a gift for Krishna, Lakshmi, Jayanthi, Jayashree or me. Every person gets one non-edible and one edible.'

Jacket: 'It is for you.'
Carrom board: 'For Jayanthi.'
Headphones: 'Krishna and Jayashree.'
Microphone: 'Lakshmi.'
Borosil teapot: 'CP.'
Roasted nuts: 'CP.'
5 Star bar: 'Jayanthi.'
Nutties: 'Lakshmi.'
Wafer biscuits: 'Jayashree.'
Chocofills: 'Krishna.'
Teddy bear: 'Me.'

The kids burst out laughing. CP looked incongruous holding it.

I told the kids, 'All boys give girls a teddy bear. I belong to the Archies generation and had always looked at the teddy bears displayed in the store longingly.

'Can you imagine Appa giving me a teddy bear? Can you imagine him *thnking* of giving me a teddy bear?

'So how to solve the problem and be happy?

'Buy the teddy bear and get him to give it to me!'

I had tried to find a teddy bear holding a sign that said 'You are sweet' or 'Thinking of you' or something like that, but Amazon did not have them and I did not have the time to go teddy bear hunting. So I settled for a chocolate brown one optimistically named 'Jam and Honey Teddy Bear'.

CP handed the teddy bear to me gravely.

I sighed and held the bear ecstatically.

Problem solved.

When my parents, my sister Vaidehi and I lived in Goa, summer holidays invariably meant going to Madurai and trying out our fragile Tamil with my grandmother. My mother often tried persuading us to learn to read and write Tamil, but it fell on deaf ears.

She spent hours diving into the vast treasures of Tamil literature and telling us stories by great Tamil writers. She told us about the writer Jayakanthan and his writings that had created a furore in those days.

One story went thus: A young girl is walking home from one village to another. On the way, an unknown man traps and sexually abuses her. The girl manages to go home and falls into her mother's arms. She weeps uncontrollably and tells her mother what happened.

Her mother listens grim-faced and takes her daughter to the bathroom. She makes her sit down and pours water on her head repeatedly. She tells her daughter, 'If you stamp on cow dung while coming home, will you cut off your foot? No, you will clean your foot and continue walking.

'In the same way, I am pouring hot water on you. That man put his filth on you. With this water I am washing it away. You are the same. Nothing has changed.'

More than three decades have passed since Amma told me this story and I can hear her voice and remember every word of it.

Every Margazhi, the *Thiruppavai* is chanted. It is a set of thirty verses in chaste Tamil composed by the young saint Andal in praise of Krishna. Never did I regret my ignorance of the Tamil language more than during my visit to the ancient temple of Srivilliputhur, dedicated to Andal. The priest chanted the *Thiruppavai* and explained the meaning. I could not understand a word because he spoke in pure Tamil.

I returned to Mumbai and persuaded a shloka teacher to teach me to chant the *Thiruppavai*. She chanted and I repeated the phrases. I was able to absorb only one word at a time. My tongue twisted over the complex pronunciations, and she would pause to correct me as I stumbled forward.

Some months later, she put her book aside and asked me to chant. With the English translation clutched in my hand, I presented the *Thiruppavai* to her. She asked me to listen to audio recordings in order to improve my pronunciation. She asked me to read the English translations so that I understood the meaning of what I was chanting.

I began chanting the *Thiruppavai* every Margazhi, early in the morning, every day. As the deep and sonorous words rolled off my tongue, I felt a great sense of kinship with my mother. I had finally made an attempt to honour my mother tongue.

At the age of five, Jayanthi began throwing objects from our terrace. To prevent this, CP installed a fine mesh everywhere except the main door of the house.

The mesh made it difficult to get the parrots in our area to come and feed at our terrace. So I had to resort to primitive methods. I 'ghusofied' green chillies and guava slices between the holes in the mesh but the parrots were not impressed.

In May 2024, all of us went on a holiday to Coonoor.

I called Anil, our driver, and persuaded him to cut a part of the mesh in the terrace to erect a parrot feeder. Anil had serious doubts about his safety because he knows how passionate CP is about his anti-Jayanthi protection mesh. I vowed to extend Z Plus security by assuming complete responsibility.

After two days I got a video from Anil.

The parrots had come!

Ten days later, we returned home. Anil pretended to be busy tending to the plants. I jumped into the fray without any ado.

'Anil, thank you! *Aapne parrots ke liye kitna achcha khane ka jagah banaya hai. Kitna high cut kiya hai mesh ko. Jayanthi jump karegi to bhi throw nahin kar sakti hai* (You have made such a good feeding area for the parrots. And you've cut into the mesh so high that even if Jayanthi jumped, she couldn't throw anything through it). Very good planning, Anil! Excellent!'

Anil, who was bent over the plants, uncoiled himself to his six feet plus height and looked at CP.

The thing is, Anil has known CP for far longer than I have. I met CP in the year 2000. Anil met him in 1993.

The two men looked at each other. Both had to contend with me—no mean thing, I assure you. They backed off.

CP, despite his custom-made, factory manufactured, durable and sustainable granite exterior, became extremely fond of the parrots. A huge sack of parrot khana was brought in.

The number of parrots swelled from two to around twenty-five or thirty. They danced alongside the huge windows and entered our home on occasions.

From my kitchen I could view them as I prepared breakfast and lunch. The sight of the rich green plumes of the parrots, their cherry red beaks, the length of their tails and their vigorous chatter filled me with joy. The entire morning was interspersed with exclamations of delight.

Of course, neither my height nor my girth permit me to climb up and fill the bird feeders. CP does it after his morning walk and feels pleased that the parrots are not scared of him anymore. They wait patiently and watch him fill the bird feeder.

A few weeks ago, I was on the phone, standing in the living room, following up on an important project. My mood was tetchy. Irritation mounted as I listened to the caller explain why something could not be done. Behind me, Jayanthi was asking for coffee. Lakshmi, for some reason, wanted my help and was clamouring, 'Mummy, Mummy.' Jayashree came out for coffee, had to pass by me to enter the kitchen, and chose to return to her room instead.

The mood was not pleasant or kind or cheerful or calm or even bearable.

I looked up. A parrot had entered our terrace and was swinging on the ledge.

I stopped and sat down.

'Sorry,' I said.

'You are more beautiful than my thoughts.

'You are more beautiful than my voice.

'You are more sane and wiser and worry about fewer things than I do.

'Sorry, that I don't smile at you anymore.

'Your beautiful green does not make my breath catch or tears crowd my throat.

'Your beauty is merged with the walls, grill, buckets, pots and pans.

'Because you are here every day, I don't value you anymore.

'I have stopped thanking the universe for you.'

I wonder how many more parrots there are in my life, ignored and taken for granted because they are there every day.

While I search for greener pastures.

I promise I will cherish the parrots on my terrace, inside my home, among my neighbours, at my workplace and every parrot who sometimes walks into our lives.

Yes, there are parrots in our lives. Adding beauty and regularity to our lives, no longer valued because we see them every day.

While we may not gasp at their beauty anymore, we can pause, smile, and recognise the green in our lives. Before moving on to search for greener pastures.

Around ten years ago, a young college student in a US college hostel died by suicide. His friend had recorded him in bed with his partner and streamed it on Twitter with the message, 'Yay! I caught him making out!'

For most of the last several months, the Indian media has been trying to fathom why a talented and seemingly successful Hindi film actor chose to take his own life.

Nineteen Minutes by the author Jodi Picoult talks about a boy who shot at a classroom full of children because his pants had been pulled down by a fellow student.

I had long conversations with Jayashree and Krishna. 'How will you deal with it, if someone humiliates you?' I asked. 'What are your options if things don't work out the way you want them to?'

When my mother passed away, she was just sixty-three years old. She had known she did not have much time left. But she wanted to live. We admitted her into a hospital. She had her back turned to us, so she did not see the doctor signalling to Appa and me to come out of the room.

The doctor did not have positive things to say. When I went back into the room, Amma whispered, 'Did she say everything is over, Sangeetha? Tell me. What did she say?' Before her discharge from the hospital, since she could not speak much, she scrawled a thank you note for the sisters in a small book and asked me to show it to them.

The night she died, she asked for a custard apple. It was her favourite fruit. I peeled away the fruit from the seed and fed it to her. She ate just a few pieces, but she enjoyed it.

She lived till her last moment. She cherished every breath she took.

I shared this story with Jayashree and Krishna. Through years of acute pulmonary disease, hooked to oxygen machines 24/7, my mother found her purpose in life through writing hundreds of blogs and stories. Even a sparrow sitting on her windowsill filled her with joy and inspired her to write.

There is no moral of the story here. I am not a wise person. I am just one among many people trying to help overcome challenges for children and trying to raise a happy and kind family.

When I got a new room in my home, I had sparrows drawn on the wall to remind me of my mother's love for life, to remind me to seek help when I need it, to remind me to seek again if I don't get help the first and second time, to ask, seek, resolve and rise again.

Provided I have help to clear up, I could make and serve dosas all day! My tomato chutney and coriander chutney have quite a fan following, let me assure you. On 'good mood, nobody has irritated me so far' days, I make a casserole full of medu vadas (not a patch on my mother's vadas though).

I often wonder who I will cook for when these four grow up. Once they start earning their own money and build their own nests, Jayashree and Krishna will not depend on me for their meals.

Lakshmi and Jayanthi will have moved into a joint family of their own: a group home for differently abled people.

Then I console myself: Jayashree and Krishna, with today's work pressures, will require help with food. If we are in the same city, I can supply dabbas. And the group home will need lots of dedicated volunteers. I imagine myself with a group of young and older adults crowding around me in the kitchen. I imagine making more varieties of chutneys, making soft dosa, thin dosa, thick dosa, crisp dosa, small dosa, big dosa for different kinds of tastes. I imagine CP stalking from table to table, making sure everyone is eating well. He will also have more people to administer 'The Look' to.

More than anything, I imagine using the simple home truths my mother taught me, that will hold good in the largest kitchen:

Be tidy when you enter the kitchen.

The person eating must feel comfortable receiving food from you.

Lighting the gas stove first thing in the morning is no less than lighting the lamp in your altar.

Offer a small prayer for everybody's well-being when you start cooking for the day.

Leave the kitchen spotless at the end of the day. You will feel so good to see a clean kitchen in the morning.

Use more hot water while preparing pongal/upma/khichdi to cut down on oil or ghee consumption.

Never exhaust the reserves in the kitchen until you buy your next lot of groceries.

Keep a couple of potatoes away for a rainy day.

Make a kitchen budget at the beginning of the month.

Learn to cook tasty meals with inexpensive ingredients. Amma used to make a tomato sabzi with green chilies that Vaidehi and I cannot replicate the taste of even to this day.

When you are serving a large group of people, dish out the vegetables into individual bowls at the start of the meal to ensure that even the last person gets a full meal.

Take out food for your helpers at the beginning of the meal and not the end. Your leftovers belong to you and not someone else.

When Amma passed on, Vaidehi and I enshrined her values in our kitchens because that's where most of our memories with our mother were made and where conversations took place.

My mother lives in the kitchen with me.

When Lakshmi was diagnosed, it was the second diagnosis of autism in the family. Unable to go home, we made our way to the Mahalakshmi temple. Surrounded by a sea of people and the

Mother Goddess herself, CP and I had never felt more alone in our lives.

While as parents, we shared distress, we did not share that distress with each other. In that too, we were alone. He was alone with his, and I was alone with mine. Finally, we had no choice but to go home.

We passed hundreds of houses on our way. So many homes right next to ours and nobody to call our own.

Water, water everywhere. Not a drop to drink.

CP's father met me one afternoon.

'When I came to Bombay with three children, I did not have a job. Then, with a lot of help from friends, I managed to get a job as a typist and five of us lived on that salary. Then, when Chakrapani was in the tenth standard, I lost my job. The family managed for two years till he cleared the twelfth standard and started going to work. Those were hard times but we made it.

'Today, you have your own hard times. You have money but you have other problems.

'Don't think I am fooled by the smile on your face. You attend all family functions. You are cheerful and happy but you have two daughters whose lives are going to be very different. They are so young. You have a long way to go. You have two more children who are young. I know how much you go through behind the smile on your face.'

By sharing his experiences, my father-in-law had made me understand that there are many birds sitting on the same tree that I was on. If one of us is hungry for food, another is deprived of love, another has more birds to feed, another is ill and another is lonely.

Recently, a family of four including a five-year-old child with autism were found dead in Bangalore. Suicide. The note left by the family talked about their financial difficulties and the challenges of a disability.

Parents and professionals and people from all walks of life are grieving and feeling wounded, imagining the family's plight. What must have gone through the parents' minds. The helpless children who did not know what was going to happen. Their trust in their parents.

There are many things that must happen to make life easier, and to open up pathways for children with disabilities and their families. Government aid. Policies and regulatory changes. Subsidies. More intervention centres. More financial aid. Counselling services.

What are the things we can do *now*? Without hesitation or delay?

Call a parent.

Call a parent and talk.

Someone to hold our hand when we feel life is slipping out of our grip.

Someone who will tell us that all is not lost, and autism is not only to be endured but to be empowered. That when there is no money in the wallet, life can be endured till better times come.

We must explore ways of having an app or a directory of around a thousand parents and more who are ready to offer free, on tap, talking services. Together Foundation is ready to establish such a service, with help.

Call a parent of someone with autism.

I am not okay. The smile on my face is not real. I need help for myself and my family.

I had saved a new kurta to wear during the last Diwali holidays. White with blue flowers. Wearing it on a chilly morning in Coorg, I was convinced that I looked like an apsara. I certainly felt like one.

I took out a matching blue dupatta and draped it for my trademark voluminous look. The shopkeeper had shown me an armful that he had taken out of a chest that looked like it had emerged from the *Pakeezah* set. '*Ek pe ek free, madam. Dupatta bechna bandh karne wale hain* (Buy one, get one free, madam. I am going to stop selling dupattas).' And like Brer Rabbit slinging a bagful of carrots on his back, I bought a bunch of dupattas and carried them home delightedly.

I went in search of my children and Aparna, the caregiver, who were waiting for me in the hotel lobby.

On the way, I met CP, who was returning from his morning walk. I twirled to the best of my ability, excitedly.

'New kurta, CP!'

'Nice!'

'Observe the blue flowers against the white background.'

'Very nice.'

'Pure white. I love white, you know, CP.'

'Shall we go for breakfast?'

'First, take my photo.'

'Okay, stand here.'

'No, I will stand against those flowers.'

'Okay.'

'Show me the photo.'

'Here.'

'It hasn't come out well. Take it again. I will stand against the green hedge.'

'Okay, wherever.'

'CP, what is this? It's not come out well.'

As I started scanning for other vistas to stand against, CP propelled me towards the lobby.

I pounced on Krishna. 'Take my photo. Appa has taken horrible ones. Please make sure they come out well.'

Click! Click! Click!

'Krishna, I look so faded!'

Jayashree: 'Here Amma, let me take the photo. Stand against the wall.'

Click!

'I am not happy!'

Aparna, the caregiver, volunteered: 'Ma'am, I will take.'

Click!

'Wow, this looks so nice! Aparna, thank you. You've made my day!'

I turned to look at my kids. 'See, you people don't know how to take a photo.'

'Amma, Aparna has used a filter!'

'Filter? What filter?'

'It makes photos look nice.'

'What about the photo you people took of my TED Talk. It was so bright and nice. There was no filter then.'

Krishna and Jayashree looked at each other. 'Amma, that photo was taken in 2016. Now it's 2022.'

I paused and looked down at the photo. I saw that the passage of seven years had taken their toll. The eyes looked a wee bit weary. The hair, instead of a vivid black, was a resounding white. The skin looked crumpled.

As I continued looking at the photo, I smiled. The eyes looked weary but shone like pools of wisdom. The hair polished to a silvery white looked reassuring. 'I am here to help you because I've walked the path you are on.' The skin looked like a ripe chikoo, ready to spread sweetness.

Yes, I have aged, and my photos will never be the same again. My smile is kinder, my head is wiser and my heart is bigger.

How do you ask your friend for help when times are tough? Do you feel awkward, inept, unequal, ashamed of taking advantage of friendship by putting a demand on it, afraid of rejection, more so when you have no gift to offer that is worthy of the friend?

Today is known as 'Kuchela dinam' in the Tamil calendar: the day poverty-stricken Kuchela (also known as Sudama) approached his beloved childhood friend for help: Krishna, whom he had not set eyes on for years and years.

Taking a cloth bag with beaten rice for the magnificent, bountiful, graceful and supreme Krishna, Kuchela could not bring himself to offer his scrawny gift. Krishna saturated Kuchela with love. Not only did he espy the bag of beaten rice, he proceeded to eat every particle with relish. Kuchela, overwhelmed by his friend's intense affection, forgot to ask for help and walked back to his village in a daze, to find his home, wife and children transformed by Krishna's love and benevolence.

All of us have both Krishna and Kuchela in us. We have the power to be humble, kind, loving and helpful to our friends in need. We have the power to have faith in our friend's love for us and knock on their door to seek help.

In my journey as a mother, I have been Kuchela again and again and again. People have been Krishnas for me and opened their doors each time I have knocked. When the winds of sorrow have blown and left my life in tangles. When the twilight of disappointment has darkened my doorstep. When the agony of autism entered my home stealthily and made a permanent place for itself amidst us. When I have tried to find sunlight in my life again. When I started looking for ways to bring the smile back onto my face. When I learnt to embrace autism as a part of my body and of my children's bodies.

Whenever I have done something positive, there has been a Krishna for this Kuchela. A Krishna who heard my knock on a dark and windy night, opened the door, gave me a hand, gave me a hug and helped me to take a foot forward.

May there always be a Krishna for every Kuchela and may every Kuchela be a Krishna to a friend in need.

One of my biggest dreams was to have a woman walk into my house in the morning and ask me, '*Aaj nashta mein kya banega* (What should I cook for breakfast)?'

This dream came true through Neelima didi, five years ago, with a condition.

She only knows how to make two vegetables: aloo and baingan.

Aloo gobhi
Aloo gobhi masala
Aloo fry
Baingan fry
Baingan masala
Bhara baingan

It's very convenient because as Tamilians, our repertoire of North Indian food revolves around aloo and gobhi. At times, when we are really out there and setting the town on fire, we ask for chilli gobhi and feel, yes, we've done it! We've asked for that one unique food that gives us an exclusive and discerning persona.

I cook two massive meals a day—breakfast and lunch. The rest is for Neelima who comes in the evening when I am usually at work. I position myself and my laptop at the dining table that functions as a huge study table and is opposite my open kitchen.

This has several advantages.

1. I can communicate with Neelima and by remote control help her make things like cabbage and palak. Plus I can keep a strict vigil on her.

    Why? She has a trademark all-encompassing master foundational recipe: take some onions, tomatoes, ginger and garlic, and make a red gold gravy with it with the help of Fortune Sunflower Oil and the Usha mixer grinder. Pour this gravy into our huge kadhai that can easily give competition to any self-respecting marriage hall. Pick up any vegetable, fry or pressure cook it, and dump it in the red gold gravy.

So before she works her magic, I get her to make the same vegetable with subtler flavours of green chilli and kadipatta and hara dhaniya, which is my master mix.

2. The other advantage of being seated at the dining table is that I can keep a vigil on the comings and goings of my grown-up children and interfere with them while maintaining the stance

of 'I don't get into my kids' space at all'. I give free tips and suggestions and ask questions:

'Jayashree, why are you studying bent over like that? Why can't you sit straight at your Pepperfry study table?'

'Lakshmi, wear a cotton stole. It's hot. This is not cotton. *Koi Lakshmi ko cotton stole dikha do* (Someone please show Lakshmi the cotton stole).'

'Jayanthi, chew your fruit. Do you think I've taken birth only to tell you this?'

3. By this time Neelima emerges from the kitchen briskly.

'*Arre Neelima, main Bangalore ja rahi hoon* (Oh, Neelima, I am travelling to Bangalore).'

'*Kab* (When)?'

'*Kal shaam ko* (Tomorrow evening).'

'*Kitne din* (How many days)?'

'*Paanch* (five).'

'*Theek hai* (Okay).'

This lady who works in our house only in the evenings comes in to cook on the days I travel. She wakes up two hours earlier on those days. One hour to fill water for her house and do other chores, and one hour for her work at my home. So she can report to work wherever she needs to, on time.

Of course, I pay for her services.

But do I pay enough for the moral support she gives me when I am away?

No.

For making Jayashree's favourite green chutney? '*Aaj uska exam hai. Maine sandwich banake diya* (Today she has exams. I made sandwiches for her).'

No.

For making tomato sabji for Jayanthi? '*Soft hai, usko achcha lagega* (It's soft, she will like it).'

No.

For gently shepherding Lakshmi out of the kitchen? '*Ruko, kuch deti hoon khane ko* (Wait, I will give you something to eat).'
No.
For going to each of my children, one by one, before leaving?
'Lakshmi, bye.'
'Jayanthi, bye.'
'Jayashree, bye. *Kuch chahiye to mala phone karo. Sab khana microwave dabba me rakha hai. Shaam ko aati hoon* (If you need something, call me. I've cooked and put everything in microwavable boxes, I will come back in the evening).'
No.

Her repertoire of two vegetables and her magic masala are as comforting to us as her kindness and the practical help that she gives us.

Give us aloo gobhi Neelima style any day.

Day 1 of the Margazhi season is dedicated to the fine actor who died young, Sridevi.

For approximately two weeks, the media sang her praises. Every day, the articles on her became smaller and smaller till one day Sridevi's demise was not newsworthy anymore. The day we stopped remembering her was the day Sridevi really died.

When my mother Mythili passed on, I was with her. That evening was the longest evening of my life. My father had gone to negotiate with the doctors for a lease of life for Amma one more time. Vaidehi, my mother's constant companion, had just returned to Bangalore. I was alone with Amma, surrounded by the hum of oxygen cylinders.

The bell rang. It was a young boy who had come with a delivery from the grocery store. I paid him and sent him off dismissively. He did not budge and looked at me solemnly with large eyes.

'Amma is not there?'
I was taken aback.

'She is not well,' I replied.

He continued, 'She has stopped coming to open the door. Can I see her?'

I silently took him inside. Amma was lying down quietly, covered with a blanket, breathing through the oxygen tubes. The boy gazed at the small lady surrounded by all this equipment. He went up to her and touched her lightly.

'Amma,' he said, and just looked at her.

She opened her eyes and smiled at him so sweetly that my heart aches and aches and aches thinking of that moment. In that one second, she once again became the teacher she had been all her life and reached out so effortlessly to that little boy. He left quietly.

Amma also left us quietly that night.

I am a Sai devotee. I console myself with an image of Sai Baba vigorously playing football on a field. He kicks the ball into the goalpost. And lo and behold! He is also the goalie! So whether on the field or off it, Amma is with him. Smiling that sweet smile. Sitting on a swing in god's fragrant garden, stringing flowers for the temple. It was something she loved doing.

I just adore my fridge. It's a huge Samsung refrigerator (if I lose around twenty kilos I could easily get in) with the freezer in the lower part and regular section in the upper part. The model is not available anymore. CP loves to say (ad nauseam) that this model was released only for the Chakrapani family and since we have now got it, we should get on with our lives and not aspire for more.

I remember from my summer holidays in my grandmother's home in Madurai that the fridge was used only to store three things: milk, curd and water.

I can't even dream of that. My entire food management system will collapse without the fridge. Cutting veggies and fruit to keep ready for the next day. Preparing chutneys, thokkus, vatha kozhambu (sambhar with a longer shelf life, made without dal) would all have to stop. Storing leftover sabzi and dal for consumption the next day. Frozen peas, frozen snacks ... the works.

In many South Indian homes, the question of storing cooked food in the fridge does not arise. Breakfast is a full course meal any time between 8 and 11 a.m., consisting of rice, sambhar and vegetables. Around 3 p.m. is coffee with a generous serving of tiffin—idli, upma or dosa.

Dinner consists of curd rice or tiffin once again, but nothing elaborate is cooked. The leftovers, particularly the bottom part of rasam, a delicious part known as 'rasam mandi', will be doled out along with whatever else had been made the entire day, leaving very little wasted.

I don't deny a sense of guilt about carrying over cooked food from one day to another. However, the crux of the issue I feel does not lie in the fridge. It lies in the entire lifestyle. Sleeping time. Waking time. More traditional Indian food. Less snacking. Very little eating out.

Today, the entire home routine is chock-a-block with real and imaginary commitments. There is always a sense of rush, a sense of little time and more things to do. Meals are not eaten together often.

Maybe we need to sit in a quiet place by ourselves and invoke the spirit of our great-grandmothers and great-grandfathers. Ask them to send pots full of simplicity and common sense our way. To understand that routine is not boring, but reassuring. Invoke our great-grandparents who will tell us, 'You know, you guys are not that bad. You guys are hardworking. You are multitaskers and take on far more responsibilities than we used to. You just need to slow down a bit. Sleep a little more at night. Eat together as a family. Cook less. Eat fresh. The fridge will take care of itself.'

My sister Vaidehi and I spent our childhood years in many places: Orissa, Hubli, Hyderabad, Poona, Goa and lastly, Delhi.

Pune, 1985: Vaidehi and I were in Class IX and Class VII, respectively, at St. Mary's School. It was a Saturday. Our parents had to go out for some work. Amma made rice, mor kozhambu (kadhi) and aloo sabzi and asked us to eat, saying she and Appa would have lunch after they returned. We ate and went into our room, reading for a while before we dozed off.

Next thing we knew, Amma was shaking us awake. She asked us to come with her and showed us the condition in which we had left the dining table. We had served ourselves the entire top layer of rice from the vessel and the serving spoon was still wedged in the remaining rice. The container with the mor kozhambu was open. The aloo sabzi was nearly finished.

Amma refused to eat and so did Appa. She taught us to keep fresh rice in the cooker for both of them and told us, 'Serve yourselves food neatly so that the person who is eating after you looks forward to eating. Make sure every vessel is covered properly and serving spoons are stacked neatly in a container. This is a home, not a hotel. Sometimes the quantity cooked may be less than is necessary. You have to ensure you leave enough for the person eating after you.'

Thirty-six years have passed. Vaidehi and I still serve ourselves rice, even if we are the only ones at home, neatly from one side of the container. When we serve food to the helpers at our home, we make the plates neatly with microwave bowls so they can have hot food. All our children make it a point to ask, 'Is there more sabzi in the kitchen? Who else has to eat?' when they serve themselves.

Amma told us, 'I am your mother. That does not mean that I don't need to eat. If you are courteous to me and Appa, you will do the same for others when you grow up.'

Even though my mother Mythili passed on in 2012, she lives with us through the values she taught us.

My mother-in-law wore a nine-yard saree 24/7 but could not figure why I did not wear jeans or skirts. She was militant. 'Is it because of my son? Tell me! You wear whatever you want.' I told her that I had tried wearing jeans only once for precisely five minutes when I was sixteen years old at the insistence of my mother, found them terribly uncomfortable and clambered out of them with relief.

She loved to attend the parties held in the building while my father-in-law would forbid her, saying it was a waste of money. From the lobby of the building, she would call me multiple times. 'Shall I stay longer? Dinner is over but they will be serving gulab jamun in some time.' Time and again, I would ask her to stay on.

Despite these sweet interactions, I don't recall sitting with her and picking up tips. Yes, I loved her. I enjoyed buying things for her. Yet, I could certainly have been a more loving and patient daughter to her.

When she passed away, I was overwhelmed with misery. I tried to assuage my feelings of guilt by thinking of the good times I had spent with her, but to no avail.

Finally, I tried to knock on the door to the other side. I spoke to tarot card readers, automatic writing experts, found out about people who help establish a connection with those who have passed on. None of these methods worked.

Then, around three years after her demise, something happened that calmed me down and forged a relationship for me with my mother-in-law beyond this earthly life.

After her demise, my mother-in-law's thick gold chain was given to me. I kept it very carefully in a locked drawer in my cupboard and rarely wore it. One afternoon, I decided to spring clean my cupboard and shifted all the things to another room. I finally went to bed at nearly midnight. I lay down with a groan. My head had barely touched the pillow when my mother-in-law's face loomed in front of me. 'Sangeetha, where is my chain?'

I sprang up with shock and rushed to the cupboard and opened the drawer. The chain was missing. I searched frantically. CP woke up. 'What happened?'

I told him but he went back to sleep. I continued searching for a couple of hours more and finally went to bed. Step by step, I rewound the day that had gone past, the multiple trips that I had made from the cupboard of one room to the cupboard of another. I woke up the next morning, pale with exhaustion.

My helper walked in. She had joined us a month earlier and had made a deep impression on me with her outbursts of anger. She used to tell me about another family she worked for and often said, 'One day I will kill them.' I had decided that she must go; it was not safe to employ her.

I took my courage in my hands and asked her, 'Did you see a gold chain anywhere around the house?'

She replied, 'No.'

I continued, 'It belonged to my mother-in-law, the only thing I have of hers. Please help me search for it.'

Something in what I said must have made an impression. After CP left for work, she brought the chain out from the folds of her clothes, gave it to me and left our home forever.

My mother-in-law had shown me in no uncertain terms that she stays with us. She had shown me that she understood my regret for not making a greater attempt to bond with her and, in the process, created a bond beyond her lifetime.

What do you do when your grown-up child does not listen to you?

He is a grown-up, right? Let him live his life.

But this grown-up child of mine, who is an adult, has autism.

So what? He still has the right of self-determination, right?

Yes, but what is self-determination without taking responsibility for consequences?

If my thirty-year-old neurotypical son wants to eat out every day, he won't ask me. He will have money of his own. If he develops health issues, he will fend for himself.

But when I won't let my thirty-year-old son with autism get dinner from a local eatery every day, he won't eat anything else. If I continue refusing him, he becomes aggressive and hits me.

If he puts on a lot of weight or becomes diabetic, taking care of him will become more difficult. So I talk to him, use social stories, and offer him alternatives in the hope that he comes around.

My son has slogged it out and cleared Class XII in the National Institute of Open Schooling. I've tried to teach him to fend for himself. Some things he has picked up. He knows how to cross the road, and I've got him a regular auto to go to his workplace. He pays the auto driver a fixed amount of money every day because he does not know how to calculate change.

His first job was at a hotel in housekeeping. I managed to enter one day and found him sweeping the floor. I was shocked because his job was to fold laundry. The others had started to tell him, '*Zara jhaadu laga do* (sweep the floor),' and he was doing it. I was so demoralised that day that I pulled him out of the job. Now he is working in an office.

One of his colleagues has a girlfriend. Every day my son comes back home and asks why he does not have a girlfriend.

Why can't he put an arm around that girl?

Of course, I would love it if he had a personal life, a sex life, a family life.

But sex comes with responsibility. With consent on both sides. Tomorrow, even if he has a partner, will my son be able to say 'no' if she touches him in a way he does not like? Will he be able to accept a 'no' from her? Will he know whom he can approach and whom he should not?

Will he be able to handle the fine nuances of understanding a person's mood and emotions without words? Will he be able to enter a relationship as an equal or will he be a boy who is wedded to a mother figure?

If my regular son were to marry and the marriage did not work, he would pick himself up eventually. If my boy with autism were to enter a sexual partnership or marriage and it didn't work, who would help him move on?

How much can I take, do and give? What about his freedom? Does it exist? Is there something called freedom in the life of a person with autism?

So we come back to square one. Can he take full responsibility for the consequences of exercising his freedom? Somebody else will have to bear the brunt of those consequences. After my lifetime, that somebody else may be a sibling or a caregiver or a group home governing body.

So I continue navigating this path, holding on to my son with an invisible leash of guided freedom. I scout for bricks all the time and build a wall of safety around my son, bit by bit. I teach him to coexist with people and build bonds. I scout for workplaces where he will be valued and empowered. I store trusted relatives and friends in the fixed deposit accounts of my mind that he will encash when I am not around, people who will give him unqualified love when I am not around. I pat him and push him and dare him to take one more step forward, one more step forward.

At night, when he goes to bed, I look at this trusting young man who has the power to fill me with joy, pull my hair out in frustration, feel like Superman one minute and completely helpless the next minute.

Autism parenting.

We wear shoes that are not available in any Bata or Hush Puppies or Nike store.

These are handmade shoes that every autism parent stitches for himself, and polishes and resoles himself before going to bed.

To be able to walk with my son, to not give up.

―――⊙⊙⊙―――

Born in the village of Kozhinjiwadi in Dharapuram, Tamil Nadu, my mother had the most idyllic childhood till she was eight years old. What stood out the most was my mother Mythili's beautiful and joyous account of her father, the village postmaster. A man who had been squeezed and thrown into the air by a python he had encountered on his way home from Rangoon, Burma. A jolly, rotund man who was generous to a fault, a man whom all the village children called Thatha, or Grandpa. A man who had a jar of 'pulippu mithai' or candy ready to give to every child who visited his home at any time. A man who, when his friend once recounted an elaborate sambhar recipe called paruppu urundai kozhambu that his wife refused to make for him, cajoled his own wife into making it for his friend that very day and giving him a memorable meal.

A man who respected people irrespective of their station in life and who would fly into a rage if domestic helpers were called 'servants'. 'Nobody is a servant,' he would say. 'She has a name. Use it when you refer to her.'

When six-year-old Mythili was caned on her palm for being naughty in class, her father refused to send her to school anymore. It was only after the teacher and principal went to his house and assured him that they would never hit any child again that Mythili went back to school.

Only eight years of pride in being her father's daughter, only eight years of the toffee jar and gobbling juicy jamuns from the school jamun tree, only eight years of wading in the waters of the cool river Amaravati and searching for smooth, polished stones to play pandi with. Only eight years before Mythili's father died in the midst of his own sixtieth birthday celebrations—celebrations that included tying the knot one more time with his wife whom he had married as a child bride before she was even ten years old.

The entire village wept for the loss of its happy, forceful, generous Postmaster Thatha.

Overnight, the family had lost its dominant earning member. Bags were packed and Mythili, her two elder brothers, sister and mother moved to Chennai, to live in a tiny one room house to start life one more time.

But to this day, the word 'servant' has never been a part of the vocabulary in either Vaidehi's or my household. To this day, when we buy lunchboxes and water bottles for our children, we set aside money for the children of our helpers. A hot meal is unfailingly served to the people who work in our homes. When the bell rings, our children carefully say, 'Amma, we have to take the garbage out,' and never ever say, 'The kachrawala has come.'

So the village postmaster lives on in the hearts and lives of the granddaughters and great-granddaughters he has never seen, through the values he taught.

The richest memories of our childhood are the stories our parents tell us about their childhood.

Family swan!

CP finds the entire family huddled around the threshold of the house, watching me struggle to get the head of the swan right in the kolam I am making. Inside the house, there are innumerable trays of cookies waiting to be baked for the chlorophyll team. Lakshmi encourages me by yelling 'Duck' at regular intervals, Krishna points to the small mountain of rangoli powder on the floor and says, 'This is from the four or five swans that Amma has attempted so far.' Jayashree says, 'Amma, this one looks more like a snake. Why don't you just draw a snake instead?' Jayanthi is gracefully perched at the window with her tab and looks like a swan herself.

CP takes a fistful of rangoli powder and proceeds to draw the swan's head. Finally, there is such a thick layer around the swan that I try to make it look better by giving it a royal blue outline.

'Once upon a time, long, long ago, there was a blue swan.'

Parents sometimes have to wait for their children to experience some simple joys. Particularly when our children have autism.

I have waited for nineteen years after Jayanthi's birth. I first waited for her to accept liquid food. Her oral motor issues made semi-solid food a horror, and solid food was out of the question for several years. I would sit with pieces of idli, bread, biscuit, roti. Put one small piece in her mouth, slide it between her teeth, place one hand on her head and the other hand below her jaw and manually chomp. She learnt to finally use her tongue and teeth to some extent.

But how much could I interfere with her? How much can I make my dreams into her dreams?

So once she learnt to eat, I stepped back and just let her be. Autism parenting is all about teaching, pushing, letting go, being at peace with what we have and letting our children be.

Sucking a mango seed was unimaginable. To hold the wet and sticky mango seed in the hand. To shape the mouth and teeth around it. To know when to stop as the seed hits against our gums and teeth. To swallow the delicious fruity bits. To feel the river of sweet joy flow down the throat.

This summer, I gave Jayanthi a plate of mango pieces. The seed was on another plate. Once she finished her mango, she sat there quietly. Hardly daring to breathe, I asked her, 'Do you want the seed?'

She nodded.

'Jayashree!' I shrieked.

'She is asking for the seed!'

Jayashree ran in and sat beside me.

We jointly invented the word 'chusofy' and gave her the seed.

'Chusofy,' Jayashree said.

'Round and round,' I said.

Jayanthi tolerated our excitement calmly and proceeded to suck the seed.

The poet John Keats has written some of the most hypnotic words in the English language in his work *Ode on Melancholy*.

> ... *Whose strenuous tongue*
> *Can burst Joy's grape against his palate fine* ...

I cannot burst into song or create a paean of verse. I can only thank the universe and Jayanthi.

I am only a mother.

Go to school in the morning.

Teachers make a big fuss of you.

Sing the school prayer.

Come out of the gate with a free Parle G biscuit packet.

Ice cream man gives you a free milk ice cream.

Eat it as if you have never seen ice cream in your life.

Get into a cycle rickshaw, dusty, happy, talking continuously.

Happy Children's Day!

Our Children's Day celebration was excruciatingly simple and joyful when I was in school in Hyderabad. The last one I recall took place when I was in Class IV, and I remember how hungry my sister and I were when we reached home. We lived in a small independent bungalow with lots of flowering plants that were my father's pride and joy. The house had a big verandah on which we spent hours playing games of make-believe and reading every comic that we could lay our hands on.

That Children's Day, we rushed home and tore out of our uniforms into home clothes, not wanting to waste a minute of our holiday. Amma served us hot rice, plain cooked dal (with *no* seasoning, just salt), some ghee and sabzi made of boiled potatoes.

We ate as if the gods were feeding us: with delight, savouring every bite. Amma stood by our side, asked if we wanted more and chatted with us as we ate lunch.

The taste of the paruppu sadam (Tamil for rice and plain dal), the flavour of the alu sabzi is on my tongue right now. Tears fill my eyes as I realise how irreplaceable a mother's love is. It is one meal that I know I will never forget and will never get to taste again.

When my father was growing up in Thanjavur, his mother would mix up leftover sambhar and keerai and boil it to a delicious consistency. The leftover rice from the previous day would have been fermented in water. She would mash the rice with curd and serve small handfuls to her children. She would ask them to make a small hole in the middle of the handful of curd rice and put in a spoon of the sambhar. The taste, my father says, cannot be described in words.

As my father and his siblings sat in a row and ate, the others noticed that my father always got that wee bit extra.

'Why?' was the militant question.

'Because,' Paati would say patiently, 'he is the eldest of ten. I have faith that he will look after all of you when we are not around and stand by you.'

Look at the faith of the mother in her son for that extra dollop of sambhar! My father has stood by his mother's conviction with his undiluted love for his siblings over many, many years, but he says he still cannot repay his mother for that extra sambhar.

The stories of my childhood would be incomplete without the stories of my parents' childhood. Simple times, home-cooked food, and a mother's faith that better times are around the corner.

When I manage to wake up early, mornings are beautiful. I make Sunrise coffee for Sai Baba, then myself. Sitting all by myself, with the breeze billowing in from all the windows, I have coffee like a queen and ruminate over my brood.

CP wanders out, holding a cup of tea with a distinct King Akbar look—I am the master of all I survey—and proceeds to water the plants while giving a running commentary on the flowers.

'We must grow ginger also,' CP opines.

'Ask Anil,' I say.

He looks rebellious and then resigned.

Anil, our driver for thirty years, has agricultural land of his own in Uttar Pradesh that he cultivates. It is he who decides what we grow in the garden and there is no pleasing him.

'*Aaj paani zyaada dala hai* (You've put too much water today).'

'Daily *paani nahi dena ka* (You should not water the plants every day)!'

'*Sukh gaye hain. Aaj paani nahin diya* (The plants are looking dry. You haven't watered them today).'

I decide to assert myself.

'Anil, *mere friend ne kaha ki tomatoes grow kar sakte hain. Aap tomato seeds lagaiye* (Anil, my friend says we can grow tomatoes. Please get the seeds).'

'*Nahin, nahin, bhabhi, tamatar nahin aayega yahan pe. Anyway, aap log jitna tamarar lete ho, woh toh Nashik ka ek pura khet lagega* (No way! Tomatoes won't grow here and anyway, your family consumes an entire field's worth of tomatoes).'

CP cackles unkindly since he is not too fond of tomatoes. I wonder where he thinks his rajma and rasam come from.

CP negotiates for unexciting vegetables like padwal and tendli and I feel vindicated when Anil refuses.

Krishna has a second line of dialogue with Anil about starting driving lessons, while Jayashree argues passionately about the banana plant.

'Where has it gone? Its leaves were so beautiful!'

'*Maine neeche building me rakha hai* (I've placed it in the building garden).'

'*Kyon, Anil bhaiya* (Why)?'

'*Jagah chahiye, idhar nahin hai* (It needs space that is not available here).'

By this time, Lakshmi has fed herself and Jayanthi with leftover chapatis with a generous smearing of Nutella.

Anil takes over.

'*Chalo, Lakshmi, Jayanthi, taiyyar ho jaiye. Centre jana hai* (Let's leave for the centre, Lakshmi and Jayanthi, get ready).'

So saying, Anil leaves the flowers he has raised in the garden and the four children he has helped us raise, and goes back to the car where he belongs.

True wealth lies in the friends, philosophers and guides we collect along the way. Anil bhaiya undoubtedly is one of them.

The children and I tested positive for Covid eleven days ago.

Krishna came to me with a pale face. 'Amma, I've tested positive.'

'Let me call up Appa's company doctor.'

'Don't panic, ma'am. Isolate him immediately. How many of you at home?'

'Five.'

'Where is Mr Chakrapani?'

'Travelling.'

'Since when?'

'Three days.'

'Okay. The remaining four of you need to get tested first thing in the morning. Tell me the names and ages please.'

'Sangeetha, forty-nine. Lakshmi, Jayanthi, Jayashree, seventeen. Excuse me, Krishna is also seventeen.'

'Are they your children, ma'am, or is it a camp or something?'

'No, no, doctor, they are quadruplets.'

'Good god! Chakrapani never told me!'

'Poor man. He is still recovering.'

'That's a good one! Okay. Can you isolate Krishna?'

Krishna quickly moved into Thatha's room and given his rich medical history, no handholding was required. I dumped a sanitiser, steam inhaler, Betadine, hot water flask, glasses and a bagful of clothes in the room, and shut the door firmly. He was on his own with his live-in partner—his mobile phone.

Jayashree packed a huge bag full of CP's clothes and went down to put it in the car while I called him. It was past 1 a.m.

'Krishna has tested Covid positive.'

In a granite block tempered with five grams of Amul butter-wala voice, CP said, 'Are you okay? What have you done with Krishna?'

'What do you mean?'

'No, no,' he said hastily. 'What I meant was, don't panic.'

'I've isolated him, if that's what your enquiry amounts to,' I said frostily.

'Okay. Okay. What about Tomato, Jayanthi and Jayashree?'

'They are in your room. I will sleep in the hall. That way I will know what is going on.'

'Tell Krishna to lock his door, or Tomato will definitely try to get in.'

'I have. CP, please don't come home when you return to Mumbai.'

'What?'

'Please don't come home. I've packed a bag—your tatty clothes, office clothes, tatty shoes, office shoes, medical file and my photo in case you miss me too much.'

'This is not the time to be funny. You will need help.'

'No. No. No. Go stay somewhere—hotel votel, anything.'

'Why?'

'Arre! Why should you get stuck in a health crisis? Plus, one of us has to be around for the kids! I am a diabetic. If I get into some kind of crisis, you will have to take over the kids.'

Silence.

Uneasy night.

At around 2 a.m., I received four images on my phone.

Positive. Positive. Positive. Positive.

CP sent our old faithful, Anil bhaiya, to stand vigil over our home from the next morning. Reporting time: 4.30 a.m. Anil bhaiya called me.

I waited till 7 a.m., then told Anil, *'Please mujhe watchman se baat karna hai* (I want to talk to the watchman).'

I told the watchman, '*Kisi ko ghar mat bhejo. Bai, dudhwala, kisi ko nahin* (Don't let anyone come to our flat. Helper, milkman, anyone).'

'Okay, madam.'

Ten hours with Krishna locked away had Lakshmi and Jayanthi looking at me like puppies with big eyes and quiet tails, and Jayashree decidedly irritable.

Lakshmi and Jayanthi were lying on either side of Jayashree. I woke them up and waited a while.

I held my palm backward against my neck. 'I am not well.'

I held my palm backward against Lakshmi's forehead. 'Lakshmi is not well.'

Then I held it against Jayanthi. 'Jayanthi is not well.'

Then Jayashree. 'Jayashree is not well.'

'We have Covid. What do we have?'

'Covid,' Lakshmi repeated dutifully.

Jayanthi can only produce the 'Oh' sound, so she supplied it helpfully.

Then all of us marched to Krishna's room and knocked at the door.

He opened the door gingerly and peeked out.

We rushed inside.

'Are you all mad?'

'No, we also have Covid!'

'Bring your flask, steam inhaler, thermometer and oximeter outside. I've ordered one more set.'

The moment Krishna came out, the atmosphere in the house lightened. Lakshmi and Jayanthi's puppy tails had small wags to them. Jayashree looked decidedly cheerful.

Though my sense of smell had gone due to Covid, that morning I could smell the fragrance and sense the strength in togetherness.

Long, long ago, when the babies had not yet entered the world, when CP and I were just a couple, so long ago that I find it hard to visualise those days, CP got our flat refurbished.

He got large French windows installed to get the best possible view of the Aarey forest and had a ledge attached to the windows—what we call 'thinnai' in Tamil.

Once the babies were born, I happily told my father-in-law, 'Let them grow up a bit, I will make them sit in a row on the thinnai and give them their snacks.'

So saying, I took out a tiny plate shaped like a saucer and handed it to CP with a couple of Marie biscuits.

My father-in-law leaned across and excitedly grabbed the saucer. 'Oh, you are using this?'

I said, 'Yes.'

'How come?'

'We have this among our vessels. I use it to serve tiny bites to eat.'

'Sangeetha, do you know, I used to eat from this plate as a child?'

Now, it was my turn to be excited.

'Really?'

'Yes, my mother used it to give me something to eat. She passed away when I was very young.'

From that day, it became my favourite plate in the house.

My kids too feel attached to the plate, but don't get as emotional about it as I do.

'Ya, Amma, we know, Amma.'

'Thatha used to eat from this plate, Amma.'

'He brought his young family from Kumbakonam to Mumbai in search of a livelihood, Amma.'

'He taught himself Carnatic music because he could not afford to learn from a music teacher, Amma.'

'He was a great believer in walking, Amma, and walked from our house to Andheri station regularly. One day, he was shocked to see you trying to get an auto to Holy Spirit Hospital and like a grandpa telling a child a story to divert attention, made conversation with you and got you to walk up to the hospital.'

'He always used to keep common medicines handy, Amma, that he gave to the needy when they had coughs and colds.'

'He spent all he had on the people who needed it the most, Amma. It was Appa who opened a bank account for Thatha and told him to start saving money.'

'He saw you making packets of prasad for a bhajan, Amma, and told you to give them to the needy instead of the people who came to attend the bhajans.'

'He never paid for special darshan or VIP darshan at a temple even when Appa started earning well, Amma. He said that the joy of seeing the lord after hours of anticipation is an unrivalled experience.'

'He wept once, Amma, because you called the garbage collector inside the house, cleaned his hand and applied a Band-Aid on the cut. He asked you to be kind always.'

'When he left for Bangalore, Amma, he paused at the departure gate and told you, 'We have never had maids or helpers in our family. Now we have two helpers living in the house to look after the children. Make sure you give them good food. Feed them first because they are dependent on you.'

'When you called him up at Bangalore and asked for permission to bring Ganpati home for Ganesh Chaturthi, he said "Sangeetha, you don't need permission to worship god."'

'When you lost your temper, Amma, and you rang him up and apologised to him, he forgave you and said, "It is you who has to keep the family together like the fingers on the hand."'

The man has passed on. The tiny plate he ate from as a little boy is more than ninety years old and ever so often, appears in one of our hands with a biscuit or a vada or a sandwich.

Ordinary possessions.

Extraordinary stories.

Give me my life back.

Give me back my youth, my hopes as a bride as I dreamed of motherhood, my sweet dreams as I waited for my children to emerge into a bright and happy world. Give me back those moments when my babies started warbling and crawling, give me those moments to show off to my neighbours and relatives how clever my babies are.

Give me back those moments when my babies started their first days in school. Let me too be one among all the mothers waiting by the school gate to hear the excited shrieks of their children as they recount their day. Take back that moment of shock and terrible acceptance of what is not to be when one of the school mums told her child, 'You must be kind to Lakshmi and Jayanthi. They are special children.'

Give me back those parties and weddings that I could not attend or when I did, had people walking on eggshells around me, avoiding talking about my children. Give me the late nights and early mornings when the family sleeps and it's just me and CP talking about our dreams and hopes for our kids.

Give me the chance to plan buying jewellery for my daughters, their first sleepover at a friend's house, talk late into the night about things that only mothers and daughters can talk about. Give me back my dreams of beautiful weddings and beautiful lives.

Yes, give me back all that I have lost, or give me a heart as mighty as a mountain, a roar as awe-inspiring as a lion's, a resolve that cannot be swerved by even a millimetre. Give me the gumption to face the life that is mine alone, let me stride forth, opening doors and windows and the tiniest vents to let light into my soul, which is darkened by sorrow.

Let me have the grace to understand that it is not about me. It is about another individual who happens to be my child. It is about the beautiful world she lives in, in which she accepts herself, and about the surprising number of things that she can learn and enjoy doing and being.

Yes, my life is not normal, and it never will be. Yes, the maker has not forgotten to give me strength and resolve, fortitude and forbearance. So give me, as Archimedes said, give me a lever long enough and a fulcrum strong enough and I will move the mountains single handed.

CP and I with (L to R) Jayashree, Lakshmi, Krishna and Jayanthi